The
MINIMALIST
Cooks DINNER

Mark Bittman

More Than

100 *Recipes*

for Fast

Weeknight Meals

and Casual

Entertaining

The MINIMALIST
Cooks DINNER

BROADWAY BOOKS | NEW YORK

Broadway Books titles may be purchased for business or promo-
tional use or for special sales. For information, please write to:
Special Markets Department, Random House, Inc., 1540 Broadway,
New York, NY 10036.

BROADWAY BOOKS and its logo, a letter B bisected on the diagonal,
are trademarks of Broadway Books, a division of Random House, Inc.

"The Minimalist" columns originally appeared in the *New York
Times*. Reprinted by permission. "The Minimalist" is a trademark
of The New York Times Company and is used under license.

Visit our website at www.broadwaybooks.com

Library of Congress Cataloging-in-Publication Data

Bittman, Mark.
    The minimalist cooks dinner: more than 100 recipes for fast
weeknight meals and casual entertaining / Mark Bittman.—1st ed.
        p.   cm.
    Includes index.
    1. Dinners and dining.   2. Quick and easy cookery.
I. Title.
TX737.B545   2001
641.5'4—dc21

FIRST EDITION

ISBN 0-7679-0671-3

10   9   8   7   6   5   4   3   2   1

For Kate and Emma

Contents

Acknowledgments

The Minimalist's place of birth and permanent home is *The New York Times,* and it is my editors there, Michalene Busico and Regina Schrambling, to whom I am most grateful. I'll always be indebted to Trish Hall and Rick Flaste, the *Times* editors who were not only responsible for the column's inception but were and remain supportive and encouraging.

The Minimalist Cooks Dinner is the work of the great folks at Broadway Books, most notably Jennifer Josephy, Steve Rubin, and Tammy Blake.

Many home cooks, fellow food-writers, and chefs all over the country and the world, have given me great ideas for "the Mini," and I've thanked them in the appropriate places. My friend Ed Schneider, whose daily correspondence challenges me and keeps me on my toes, and my coauthor Jean-Georges Vongerichten—a minimalist's maximalist—deserve special mention.

Thanks as usual to Angela Miller, who is always there for me, not only as an agent but as a friend; to the ever-tolerant John Willoughby; and to the loving Alisa Smith. And, especially this year, I was blessed to count among my friends David Paskin, Pamela Hort, John Ringwald, Semeon Tsalbins, Joe and Kim McGrath, Bill Shinker and Susan Moldow, Mitchell Orfuss, Naomi Glauberman, John Bancroft, Madeline Meacham, Fred Zolna, and Sherry Slade. Karen Baar was the source of a large chunk of the inspiration and creativity that goes into the Minimalist; for this and many other things I'll always be grateful.

—Mark Bittman

Introduction

These hundred-odd recipes represent about two years of my *New York Times* column, an average of a recipe a week. They have a couple of things in common. First of all, that they were developed at the rate of one a week is no coincidence, since almost all appeared in my weekly column, "The Minimalist." Second, they are intended to be easy, often simple, and usually quick (those that are not quick spread out a little bit of work over a few hours).

If they are successful, if they provide you with satisfying dishes with a minimum of effort, it's thanks in large part to the fact that I am lucky enough to work on just one recipe a week. There were times in my career as a food writer when I was obligated to come up with twelve recipes a week; this simply cannot be done on a regular basis without begging and borrowing recipes from friends, chefs, and fellow food writers, and submitting them without testing or changing.

I still beg and borrow ideas, and from the same sources. But these days I take those ideas home, to my average suburban kitchen with its average equipment, and work them to death, until I'm satisfied that they can't be made any simpler or easier without sacrificing too much of their essence.

If this sounds like a compromise, it is. Cooking, like most everything else in life, is exactly that. We never have as much time as we like, we rarely have the perfect ingredients, and few of us—myself included, lest you doubt it— have the skills to measure up to truly demanding recipes. My job, as I see it, is to show you the little path I blaze, the route that makes things faster, more flexible, and easier.

Sometimes I am accused of going too far, and failing to retain a recipe's soul, losing too much of its vitality in the process of simplifying it. I try to take this objection into account and remedy it by offering a wide range of substitutions and variations, ways to make recipes more complex, slightly fancier, more sophisticated, or just different.

Simple, as a friend of mine said to me, need not mean simple-minded. As much thought and work may go into figuring out a great three-ingredient, 30-minute recipe as one that includes thirty ingredients and takes 3 hours. The fact that the preparation and execution is faster and easier does not make the recipe less sophisticated, complex, or desirable—indeed, it may make it more so.

The Minimalist Cooks Dinner differs from its predecessor, *The Minimalist Cooks at Home*, in a few ways. The texts are shorter, the pointer sections more substantial. Furthermore, I have included serving and wine suggestions as well as a chapter of quick, easy side dishes, so that you can easily complete a meal based on one of the recipes here. But I want to stress that these serving suggestions are exactly that—a list of dishes that I think might well serve to complement the main course. You might want more, less, different, or none, and by all means I encourage you to go your own way.

That's what home cooking is about.

The
MINIMALIST
Cooks DINNER

Soups and Stews

Vichyssoise with Garlic

TIME: 40 to 60 minutes, plus time to chill

MAKES: 4 servings

In its traditional form, this cold potato-and-leek soup borders on boring: potatoes, leeks (or onions, or a combination), water or stock, salt and pepper, butter, and cream. What little complexity the soup has comes from lightly browning the vegetables in the butter, using lots of salt and pepper, good stock, and, of course, the cream. But if you add other vegetables, like garlic and carrots, things become more interesting. And you can nudge the soup over into gazpacho territory by adding a tomato to the mix, along with basil. Some protein, like shrimp, makes it even more of a whole-meal soup.

4 cups water, stock, or a combination

1 pound potatoes, peeled and cut into slices or chunks

1 pound leeks or onions or a combination (leeks well-washed and onions peeled), cut into slices or chunks

1 whole head green garlic, plus its stem, chopped into pieces, or 3 garlic cloves, peeled

Salt and freshly ground black pepper

½ to 1 cup heavy cream or half-and-half

Chopped parsley, chervil, or chives

1 Combine the water, or stock, potatoes, leeks, garlic, salt, and pepper in a saucepan, cover, and turn the heat to high. Bring to a boil, then lower the heat so the mixture simmers steadily but not violently. Cook until the potatoes are tender, 20 to 30 minutes. Cool or chill, then season to taste.

2 Purée in a blender, then chill fully. Stir in the cream, then taste and adjust the seasoning and serve, garnished with parsley.

WINE Good Chardonnay, preferably Chablis

SERVE WITH 60-Minute Bread (page 207) or good store-bought bread

BE FLEXIBLE AND GO with what is available. The basic technique is sound and universal: Cook the vegetables in water or stock, then cool, puree, and chill. The initial browning in butter makes a pleasant but not highly significant difference, so I skip it.

IF YOU CAN GET young (green) garlic, use it, and in quantity. Otherwise substitute regular garlic.

IF YOU HAVE homemade stock, by all means use it; it will add a great deal of complexity. But if the option is canned stock or water, this is a place to save your money: Use water.

Vichyssoise with Tomato and Basil: Core 2 medium tomatoes (cut a cone-shaped wedge out of the stem ends), then cut them in half horizontally. Squeeze and shake out the seeds, then cut the tomatoes into chunks. Substitute the tomatoes for the garlic and proceed as above. Purée with about 20 washed basil leaves. Do not use cream. To serve, garnish with chopped basil.

Vichyssoise with Carrot: Peel and chop 4 medium carrots, and add to the liquid, along with the potatoes and leeks (garlic is optional but still good). Add 1 cup more liquid and proceed as above, puréeing, stirring in cream and garnishing with parsley.

Simply add some cold grilled or steamed shrimp or cubed cooked chicken to the soup before serving.

Nearly Instant Miso Soup with Tofu

TIME: About 15 minutes
MAKES: 4 servings

This ultra-simplified miso soup is delicious and, if the reigning wisdom is correct, good for you because it is soy-based. It can be used in place of stock in many recipes, although you have to take care, because it has much more character than most stocks.

"Real" Miso soup is a little more complicated, and begins with dashi, a basic Japanese stock made with kelp (kombu) and flakes of dried bonito (a relative of tuna). I simply whisk or blend a tablespoon of miso into a cup of water, and turn the soup into a meal by adding cubed tofu and some vegetables at the last moment. Instead of tofu, you might cook shrimp or boneless chicken in the soup for a couple of minutes.

⅓ cup dark miso

½ pound any tofu, cut into ½-inch cubes

¼ cup minced carrots

¼ cup minced scallions

1 Bring 6 cups water to a boil in a medium saucepan. Turn the heat to low, then mix about ½ cup of water with the miso in a bowl or blender; whisk or blend until smooth. (If you have an immersion blender, the fastest and easiest tool here, carry out this operation in a tall measuring cup.)

2 Pour the miso mixture back into the hot water and add the tofu and carrots; stir once or twice and let it sit for a minute, just long enough to heat the tofu through. Add the scallions and serve.

WINE Sake or not-too-dry Riesling

SERVE WITH Easy Rice (page 204); grilled tofu or chicken breasts brushed with soy sauce

BUY TRADITIONAL, unpasteurized, even organic miso, which is common enough, inexpensive enough (it's tough to spend more than eight dollars on a pound of miso), and better than quick-made miso, which is comparable to quick made parmesan or wine. All miso has a long shelf-life, keeping for at least several months in the refrigerator with little or no loss of quality.

TRADITIONALLY, thick, dark brown hatcho miso is used to make soup; but the lighter varieties, which are more often used to make dressings and sauces, are fine as well.

FIGURE ABOUT 1 tablespoon of miso per cup of water, which means about ⅓ cup to serve four people: you may like the soup more or less intensely flavored, though the tendency is to use too much miso. The only trick lies in getting the miso to dissolve properly, creating a smooth, almost creamy soup rather than a lumpy one. But this is in fact a snap: You just whisk or blend the miso with a few tablespoons of hot water before adding the rest of the liquid. Any cooking from that point on must be gentle to preserve the miso's flavor and aroma.

Instant Miso Soup for One: Put 1 tablespoon miso in a mug. Add a couple of tablespoons of boiling water and whisk or stir until smooth. Fill the cup with hot water.

Miso Soup with Shrimp or Chicken: Substitute ½-inch cubes of peeled (and deveined, if you like) shrimp or boneless, skinless chicken for the tofu. Cook for 2 minutes, or until nearly done. Add the carrots and, when the soup is done, the scallions.

The Minimalist's Corn Chowder

Anyone who's ever had a garden or raided a cornfield knows that when corn is young you can eat it cob and all, and that the cob has as much flavor as the kernels. That flavor remains even when the cob has become inedibly tough, and you can take advantage of it by using it as the base of a corn chowder—a corn stock, if you will. Into that stock can go some starch for bulk, a variety of seasonings from colonial to contemporary, and, finally, the corn kernels. The entire process takes about a half hour, and the result is a thick, satisfying chowder that is best made in late summer.

4 to 6 ears corn

1 tablespoon butter or neutral oil, like canola or grapeseed

1 medium onion, chopped

2 medium potatoes, peeled and chopped

Salt and freshly ground black pepper

2 tomatoes, cored, seeded, and chopped, optional

1 cup milk

½ cup chopped fresh parsley leaves, optional

1 Shuck the corn and use a paring knife to strip the kernels into a bowl. Put the cobs in a pot with 4 cups water; bring to a boil, cover, and simmer for 10 minutes.

2 Meanwhile, put the butter or oil in a saucepan and turn the heat to medium-high. When the butter melts or the oil is hot, add the onion and potatoes, along with a sprinkling of salt and pepper. Cook, stirring occasionally, until the onion softens, about 5 minutes; add the tomatoes if you're using them and cook, stirring, for another minute or two.

3 After the corn cobs have cooked for at least 10 minutes, strain the liquid into the onion-potato mixture. Bring to a boil, then turn the heat down so the mixture simmers. When the potatoes are tender, about 10 minutes, add the corn kernels and milk and heat through. Taste and adjust seasoning if necessary, garnish with the parsley, and serve.

WINE Pinot Grigio, Sauvignon Blanc, or any fresh, crisp white

SERVE WITH Simple Green Salad (page 196), or any green salad, or Tomato Salad with Basil (page 198)

STRIP THE KERNELS from the cob with a sharp knife, and make sure to catch any liquid that seeps out during the process.

TO MINIMIZE COOKING TIME, chop the potatoes into ¼-inch pieces. Leave them larger if you're not in a hurry.

AS LONG AS your corn is young and tender, the kind you can just about eat raw, the kernels should be held out of the mix until the chowder is just about ready, so they don't overcook. But the new supersweet hybrids, which retain much of their flavor in the refrigerator for a few days, are not as tender, and their kernels should be cooked for a few minutes at least. Just keep tasting and stop cooking when the texture seems right.

Corn Chowder with Bacon and Cream: In step 2, substitute ½ cup chopped bacon for the butter or oil; cook over medium heat until it renders some of its fat, then add the onion. Proceed as above. In step 3, use heavy cream or half-and-half in place of milk.

Curried Corn Chowder: In step 2, use oil and add 1 tablespoon curry powder, or to taste, and 1 tablespoon peeled and minced ginger to the onions as they cook. Proceed as above. In step 3, use sour cream in place of milk; garnish with minced cilantro in place of parsley.

If you use the tomatoes, you can also leave out the milk (think of it as "Manhattan corn chowder").

Cucumber Soup, Two Ways

For years I was stuck on blended or cooked cucumber soups, until I was served a clear, chunky, ice-cold soup laced with soy and the sour-sweet-salty-spicy combination characteristic of so much Southeast Asian cooking. After I duplicated that, it occurred to me to make a similar preparation with nam pla (fish sauce) and coconut milk, an equally spicy but wonderfully creamy concoction. I doubt I'll ever use either the blender or the stove to make cucumber soups again.

Asian-Style Cucumber Soup

3 cups chicken stock, preferably chilled

2 medium cucumbers

3 tablespoons soy sauce

2 tablespoons rice or white
  wine vinegar

1 small chile, stemmed,
  seeded, and minced, or ¼
  teaspoon cayenne, or to
  taste

2 teaspoons sugar

½ cup minced trimmed scallions, both white and green
  parts

1 cup washed and chopped
  watercress or arugula,
  optional

1 cup washed and roughly
  chopped cilantro, mint, Thai
  basil, or a combination

1 If the chicken stock is not cold, throw it in the freezer while you prepare the cucumbers. Peel them, then cut them in half the long way; use a spoon to scoop out the seeds. Slice them as thinly as possible (a mandoline is ideal for this). Mix them in a bowl with the soy sauce, vinegar, chile, and sugar and let them sit, refrigerated, for about 20 minutes.

2 Add the stock, scallions, and watercress or arugula if you like, and stir. Taste and adjust the seasoning, then chill or serve. Just before serving, garnish with the herbs.

WINE With the Asian-style soup, a fruity Riesling or Gewürztraminer; with the European-style soup, a crisp Graves or Sauvignon Blanc

SERVE WITH With the Asian-style soup, Rice Salad with Peas and Soy (page 200) or any grain salad. With the European-style soup, Olive Oil Croutons (page 208) or any good bread

European-Style Cucumber Soup

1½ cups chicken stock, preferably chilled

2 medium cucumbers

Salt and freshly ground black pepper

1½ cups yogurt, preferably full-fat

2 shallots, peeled and minced, or about ¼ cup minced red onion or scallion

1 cup washed and chopped watercress, optional

1 cup washed and roughly chopped dill or mint

1 If the chicken stock is not cold, throw it in the freezer while you prepare the cucumbers. Peel them, then cut them in half the long way; use a spoon to scoop out the seeds. Slice them as thinly as possible (a mandoline is ideal for this). Mix them in a bowl with 2 teaspoons salt and let sit, refrigerated, for about 20 minutes.

2 Add the stock, black pepper, yogurt, shallots, and watercress, if you like, and stir. Taste and adjust the seasoning, then chill or serve. Just before serving, garnish with the herbs.

Keys To SUCCESS

THE TIME SPENT in making these soups lies mostly in chilling: Refrigerate the cucumbers as their moisture is drawn out; refrigerate the stock, yogurt, or sour cream that is their base; and, if time allows, refrigerate the soup itself so you can serve it really cold.

THE LIVELY FLAVOR of these soups derives largely from a load of herbs—you can vary them, but don't omit them.

With MINIMAL Effort

ASIAN-STYLE CUCUMBER SOUP

Cucumber-Coconut Soup: Substitute 2 cups coconut milk and 1 cup water for the stock and, if you have it, nam pla (Thai fish sauce) for the soy sauce.

| Add some precooked shrimp to the soup just before serving.

EUROPEAN-STYLE CUCUMBER SOUP

| Substitute sour cream for the yogurt (you can use water in place of chicken stock if you like). Add the juice of ½ lemon to the cucumbers while they sit in the salt.

| Toss some cooked, shredded chicken meat into the soup before serving.

Roasted Chestnut Soup

Chestnuts have a subtle but distinctive flavor; another, less-well-known attribute is their ability to lend a rich, creamy texture to anything in which they're pureed—making cream completely superfluous. This soup is a perfect example, and if you can find frozen, peeled chestnuts, it's the work of a moment. But even if you cannot, the chestnut-peeling process takes about 20 minutes start to finish, and much of that time is unattended; you can use it to chop and cook the vegetables.

10 large chestnuts, peeled or unpeeled

2 tablespoons extra virgin olive oil or butter

2 cups chopped celery

½ cup chopped onion

Salt and freshly ground black pepper

4 cups good chicken stock

Chopped celery leaves or parsley

1 If you have peeled chestnuts, proceed to step 2. If your chestnuts still have their skins, preheat the oven to 350° F. Use a sharp (preferably curved) paring knife to make an "X" on their flat sides. Bake them in an open pan for 10 to 15 minutes, or until their peels begin to open away from the meat. They will then be easy to peel; remove both outer and inner skins while they are warm. (The peeled chestnuts will cook faster if you chop them roughly, but it isn't necessary.)

2 Meanwhile (if you have peeled chestnuts, start here), pour the olive oil into a deep skillet or casserole, turn the heat to medium, and heat for a couple of minutes. Add the celery, onion, and a good sprinkling of salt and pepper. Cook, stirring occasionally, until the onion is translucent, about 10 minutes. Add the stock and the chestnuts, bring to a boil, and partially cover. Adjust the heat so that the mixture simmers and cook until the chestnuts are mushy, about 30 minutes.

3 Carefully purée the soup in a blender (if you are not in a hurry, cool it slightly first for extra caution). Measure and add sufficient water to total 6 cups of liquid. Reheat, adjust the seasoning if necessary, garnish, and serve.

WINE Bordeaux or another big red

SERVE WITH 60-Minute Bread (page 207) or good store-bought bread; Roasted Peppers (page 195); Glazed Carrots (page 201)

STARTING FROM SCRATCH with whole chestnuts is preferable, because they gain a bit of flavor as you toast them lightly to remove the skins.

CERTAINLY GOOD STOCK is helpful; but even when made with decent canned stock, this soup has guts.

Chestnut Soup with Bacon: Start by rendering ¼ cup or so of diced slab bacon; scoop out the solids and reserve them for a garnish. Then sauté the celery and onion in the rendered fat and proceed as above.

Chestnut Soup with Shiitake: Garnish the soup with a cup or so of shiitake mushrooms (caps only), sliced and sautéed in butter or oil until lightly browned.

Black-Eyed Pea Soup with Ham and Greens

The soup draws its main flavors from olive oil, cured meat, and watercress. It gains substance and supporting flavors from the peas and a little onion. The combination is delicious, warming, and celebratory in a rustic way. Equally important is that it opens the door to a world of possibilities, since you can substitute for any or all of the principal ingredients without missing a step—see With Minimal Effort.

Black-Eyed Pea Soup with Ham and Watercress

2 tablespoons extra virgin olive oil

2 ounces ham or prosciutto, chopped

1 medium onion, chopped

2 cups cooked, canned, or frozen black-eyed peas

2 cups watercress, washed, trimmed, and chopped

Salt and freshly ground black pepper

1 Pour 1 tablespoon of the oil into a deep skillet or casserole and turn the heat to medium-high. Add the meat and cook, stirring, for a minute; then add the onion and cook, stirring occasionally, until it softens and begins to brown, about 10 minutes. Add the peas and 4 cups water and bring to a boil; turn the heat to medium-low and simmer, uncovered, until the peas are completely tender—10 minutes for cooked or canned black-eyed peas, about 30 minutes for frozen.

2 Stir in the watercress and cook, stirring occasionally, for just a couple of minutes, or until it wilts. Add more water, if necessary. Taste and adjust the seasoning, stir in the remaining 1 tablespoon oil, and serve.

WINE Chianti or another light red
SERVE WITH Cornbread (page 209), 60-Minute Bread (page 207), or good store-bought bread

FROZEN BLACK-EYED PEAS (and white beans, chickpeas, and others) can be found in the supermarket freezer, and their convenience and quality are unparalleled; they're faster and easier to use than dried beans or peas and far better-tasting than canned ones. In the case of black-eyed peas, they need about half an hour of cooking to become fully tender. If you use pre-cooked peas or those from a can (please rinse them first), the cooking time will be reduced to almost nothing.

| The meat can be prosciutto or ham; you can use bacon or pancetta instead, but cook them a little longer.

| Instead of onion, you can use garlic, leek, or shallots.

| Black-eyed peas are the traditional choice, but any legume will work perfectly well.

| For the watercress, substitute arugula or spinach, or any winter green, like kale, mustard, collards, and turnips, all of which will take a little longer to cook—add them to the soup along with the peas.

| Liquid condiments, like Tabasco or another hot sauce or vinegar, are good here.

| Increase the amount of meat to ½ pound or so (this is especially good with ham), double the amount of greens, and cook the soup until it's thick; you can call it a stew.

Chickpea Soup, with or without Meat

The cooking liquid of chickpeas, unlike that of most other beans, is so good-tasting that it makes the basis of a great soup, seasoned with garlic, herbs, and some aromatic vegetables, for example. Purée some of the cooked chickpeas, then stir them back into the soup, and it becomes deceptively, even sublimely, creamy.

Chickpea Soup with Sausage

1½ cups dried chickpeas

5 garlic cloves, peeled and cut into slices

3 sprigs rosemary or thyme

1 medium to large carrot, cut into small dice

1 celery stalk, peeled and cut into small dice

1 medium onion, cut into small dice

Salt and freshly ground black pepper

1 teaspoon minced garlic

½ pound Italian or garlic sausage, grilled or broiled and cut into thin slices, optional

1 tablespoon extra virgin olive oil, or to taste

1 If you have the time, soak the chickpeas for several hours or overnight in water to cover (if not, don't worry). Combine the chickpeas, sliced garlic, and herbs in a large saucepan with fresh water to cover by at least 2 inches. Bring to a boil, turn down the heat, and simmer, partially covered, for at least 1 hour, or until fairly tender. Add additional water if necessary, and skim any foam that rises to the top of the pot.

2 Scoop out the herbs and add the carrot, celery, onion, salt, and pepper to the pot. Continue to cook until the chickpeas and vegetables are soft, at least another 20 minutes. Remove about half the chickpeas and vegetables and carefully purée in a blender with enough of the water to allow the machine to do its work. Return the purée to the soup and stir; reheat with the minced garlic, adding additional water if the mixture is too thick.

3 Stir in the sausage and cook a few minutes longer. Taste and adjust the seasoning, then serve, drizzled with the oil.

WINE Chianti, a red from the South of France, or any other light but assertive red

SERVE WITH 60-Minute Bread (page 207), good store-bought bread, or Olive Oil Croutons (page 208); Roasted Peppers (page 195)

THIS RECIPE will work with canned chickpeas, but some adjustments are necessary; see With Minimal Effort.

LIKE ANY BEAN, chickpeas can be cooked without soaking, though they will cook somewhat more quickly if they are soaked for 6 to 12 hours beforehand. Soaked or not, the cooking time for beans is somewhat unpredictable, depending largely on how much moisture they have lost during storage (older beans, being drier, require longer cooking times). Generally speaking, soaked chickpeas will take about 1½ hours to become tender; unsoaked ones will take about 30 minutes longer.

| To use canned chickpeas, rinse 4 cups chickpeas and combine with 6 cups chicken or vegetable stock and the vegetables as in step 2 above. Cook until the vegetables are tender, then proceed as above.

| Omit the sausage, or substitute leftover bits of cooked chicken, beef, pork, or lamb. Or cook something especially for the soup, like shrimp or more vegetables.

Cauliflower Curry with Chicken

TIME: 40 minutes
MAKES: 4 servings

There's a more-or-less standard Indian dish of cauliflower and potatoes that to me, despite its lovable flavors, is simply too starchy. Substitute boneless chicken for the potatoes, however, and the preparation turns into a one-dish meal, increasing both its appeal and its usefulness. The chewiness of the chicken—as opposed to the mealiness of the potatoes—gives the dish an added dimension.

2 tablespoons peanut, grape-seed, or other oil

½ cup minced onion

1 head cauliflower (about 2 pounds)

1 tablespoon cumin seeds, optional

2 teaspoons curry powder, or to taste

5 or 6 canned plum tomatoes, with their juice

Salt and freshly ground black pepper

1 pound boneless, skinless chicken, cut into ½-inch cubes

Juice of 1 lemon) *better without*

Minced fresh parsley or cilantro, optional

1 Pour the oil into a 12-inch skillet and turn the heat to high; add the onion and cook, stirring occasionally, until it begins to brown, about 5 minutes. While the onion is cooking, trim the cauliflower and cut the florets into ½-inch-thick pieces.

2 When the onion has browned a little, add the cumin seeds and curry and cook for about 30 seconds. Add the cauliflower and stir, still over high heat, for another minute. Cut up the tomatoes and add them, along with their juice, ¼ cup water, and a generous sprinkling of salt and pepper. Cover and turn the heat to medium-low.

3 Cook for 10 minutes, stirring once or twice, or until the cauliflower is beginning to become tender. Add the chicken, stir, cover, and cook for another 6 to 8 minutes, until the chicken is cooked through. (If the sauce threatens to dry out at any point, add a little more water.) Stir in the lemon juice, taste and adjust the seasoning, garnish with parsley, if you like, and serve.

If making ahead and reheating, don't cook as long so cauliflower doesn't get too soft and mushy.

WINE Beer or Zinfandel or another light, assertive red

SERVE WITH Any flatbread or Easy Rice (page 204)

THE CUMIN will gain flavor if you toast it first: Put it in a small, dry skillet over medium heat and cook, shaking the pan occasionally, until it is fragrant.

| Substitute potatoes, peeled and cut into ½-cubes, for the chicken; make sure they're cooked through before serving.

| To the cooking onion, add 1 tablespoon or even more of minced ginger; 1 to 2 teaspoons of minced garlic; some fresh or dried chiles, or 1 to 2 pinches cayenne.

| Whether you're using chicken or potatoes, 2 cups of cubed eggplant cooked with the cauliflower is a great addition.

Curried Tofu with Soy Sauce

TIME: 20 to 30 minutes
MAKES: 4 servings

Over the years, almost despite myself, I have become increasingly fond of tofu, not for its flavor—which is so subtle as to be almost nonexistent, especially in a full-flavored dish like this one—but for its silken, creamy texture. (Its reported health benefits don't hurt, but who knows whether these will be borne out in the long run?) But given that tofu does not add much body to a dish, you need a substantial sauce, like one with canned coconut milk as its base. Like heavy cream, coconut milk will thicken a sauce, making it luxurious in almost no time.

2 tablespoons peanut, grape-seed, or other oil

1 large onion, minced

1 tablespoon curry powder, or to taste

1 cup roughly chopped walnuts or unsalted cashews

One 12- to 14-ounce can (1½ to 2 cups) unsweetened coconut milk or 2 cups homemade coconut milk

1 block tofu (about 1 pound), cut into ¾-inch cubes

2 tablespoons soy sauce, or to taste

Salt

Cayenne

1 Put the oil in a 10- or 12-inch nonstick skillet, turn the heat to medium-high, and heat for 1 minute. Add the onion and cook, stirring occasionally, until the edges of onion pieces are well-browned, about 10 minutes (for best flavor, the onions must brown but not burn). Add the curry powder and cook, stirring, for 30 seconds or so; add the nuts and cook, stirring occasionally, for about 1 minute.

2 Add the coconut milk. Stir, bring to a boil, and reduce the heat to medium. Add the tofu, stir, and let the tofu heat through for about 3 minutes. Stir in the soy, then taste and adjust the seasoning with soy, salt, and/or cayenne as necessary. Serve.

WINE Not-too-dry Riesling or Gewürztraminer
SERVE WITH Easy Rice (page 204) and, if you like, Steamed Broccoli (or Other Vegetable) (page 203)

THE ONIONS must be browned carefully and thoroughly: Keep the heat high enough so that this happens in timely fashion—it should take about 10 minutes, and in no case more than 15—but not so high that the onions burn. I call this level of heat "medium-high," but since all stoves are different it will require some judgment. The oil should be bubbling but not smoking, and you must stir the onions every minute or so. After 3 or 4 minutes they should begin to brown, and they are done when their edges are quite dark and their interiors somewhat darkened.

TO MAKE your own coconut milk, combine 2 cups grated unsweetened coconut and 2 cups boiling water in a blender; let cool a bit, then blend carefully, taking care that the hot liquid does not splatter. Strain and discard solids.

For the tofu, substitute ½-inch cubes of chicken, shrimp, or pork; cook in the sauce until done, about 5 minutes.

Whole-Meal Chicken Noodle Soup, Chinese Style

Fresh Asian-style noodles are turning up everywhere these days—even supermarkets—and they're ideal for soups, because you can cook them right in the broth. It only takes a few minutes and, unlike dried noodles, they won't make the broth too starchy. Here, then, is a noodle-based chicken soup that you can take in many different directions.

6 cups chicken stock

10 ginger slices

2 garlic cloves, peeled and lightly crushed

1 tablespoon peanut or vegetable oil

1 teaspoon minced garlic

1½ cups chopped cooked chicken

1 cup broccoli florets, cut into 1-inch or smaller pieces

1 pound fresh thin egg noodles (may be labeled "soup noodles" or "wonton noodle" or simply "noodles")

2 tablespoons soy sauce, or to taste

1 tablespoon toasted sesame oil

½ cup minced scallions

1 Heat the stock with the ginger and crushed garlic while you prepare the other ingredients. Keep it warm and simmering until you are ready to use it.

2 Pour the peanut oil into a broad, deep skillet or saucepan and turn the heat to medium-high. Add the minced garlic and stir, then add the chicken. Turn the heat to high and cook, stirring only occasionally, until the chicken begins to brown, about 5 minutes. Add the broccoli and cook, stirring occasionally, for about 5 minutes.

3 Strain and add the stock; adjust the heat so that it boils gently. Add the noodles and cook, stirring occasionally, until they are separate and tender, about 3 minutes. Stir in the soy sauce and sesame oil, then taste and adjust the seasoning. Divide the soup among four bowls; add a little more stock to each if you want the mixture soupier. Garnish with the scallions and serve.

WINE Dry (fino) sherry or beer

SERVE WITH I don't call it "whole-meal" soup for nothing

START WITH canned chicken stock if you must, but don't skip the step of simmering it briefly with the garlic and ginger, which will give it a decidedly Chinese flavor.

DO NOT OVERCOOK the noodles. If you use thin ones, they'll be ready almost immediately after you add them to the simmering stock.

| Add a dried chile to the stock along with the ginger and garlic.

| For the chicken, substitute diced Chinese sausage, or diced raw or roast pork, or roast duck; or use a combination.

| For the broccoli, substitute snow or snap peas or green beans, or use a combination. Minced carrots are also good.

Fast Mushroom Soup, Creamy or Low-Fat

TIME: 30 to 45 minutes
MAKES: 4 servings

Even as they become increasingly common, there remains something special, even exotic, about mushrooms. And combining their various forms allows you to make a splendid and impressive soup in less than half an hour. The choices you make determine whether you have a light-tasting, low-fat, dark soup or a rich, creamy, traditional soup. In the first, you use olive oil, tomatoes, and parsley. In the second, butter and cream—though not outrageous amounts of either. The soups are both delicious and quite different from one another.

Fast, Creamy Mushroom Soup

2 ounces dried mushrooms (about 1 cup)

2 tablespoons (¼ stick) unsalted butter

6 to 8 ounces fresh mushrooms, trimmed and sliced

Salt and freshly ground black pepper

2 tablespoons minced shallots

Water or stock

1 cup heavy cream

2 teaspoons fresh lemon juice, or to taste

Chopped chervil or parsley, optional

1 Combine the dried mushrooms in a saucepan with 5 cups water; bring to a boil, cover, turn the heat to low, and simmer for about 10 minutes, or until tender.

2 Meanwhile, put the butter in a skillet and turn the heat to medium-high. When the butter melts, add the sliced fresh mushrooms and turn the heat to high. Cook, stirring occasionally and seasoning with salt and pepper, until they give up their liquid and begin to brown. When the dried mushrooms are tender, scoop them from the liquid with a slotted spoon and add them to the skillet, along with the shallots. When all the fresh mushrooms are browned and the shallots are tender, about 3 minutes later, turn off the heat.

WINE Dry sherry would be ideal, or a big, rich Chardonnay from Burgundy or California

SERVE WITH A rich soup that, with 60-Minute Bread (page 207) or good store-bought bread and Simple Green Salad (page 196), could be a meal. Or follow it with a light main course of chicken or fish.

3 Strain the mushroom-cooking liquid through a cheesecloth-, napkin-, or towel-lined strainer; measure it and add water or stock to make sure there are at least 4 cups. Rinse the saucepan and return the liquid to it. Add the mushrooms and cream and heat through; taste and adjust the seasoning. Add the lemon juice, taste once more, garnish with chervil if you like, and serve.

Keys To SUCCESS

SIMMERING DRIED MUSHROOMS produces a flavorful broth, but it must be strained well to remove any traces of grit.

THE BEST-TASTING dried mushrooms are dried porcini (also called cèpes), which have come down about 50 percent in price over the last few years. Or you can start with inexpensive dried shiitakes, readily available in Asian markets (where they're also called black mushrooms), or any other dried fungi, or an assortment.

AN ASSORTMENT of fresh mushrooms is best, but you can simply rely on ordinary button (white) mushrooms or shiitakes (whose stems, by the way, are too tough to eat).

With MINIMAL Effort

FAST, CREAMY MUSHROOM SOUP
| In step 3, add the cream and half the mushrooms to the mushroom liquid and purée. Reheat and garnish with the remaining mushrooms, heating them through before serving.

FAST, LOW-FAT MUSHROOM SOUP
| Cook 1 chopped medium onion, or 3 or 4 chopped shallots along with the fresh mushrooms in step 2.

Fast, Low-Fat Mushroom Soup

2 ounces dried mushrooms
(about 1 cup)

2 tablespoons extra virgin
olive oil

6 to 8 ounces fresh mush-
rooms, trimmed and sliced

Salt and freshly ground black
pepper

2 teaspoons minced garlic

1 cup diced tomatoes (canned
are fine; don't bother to
drain)

Water or stock

Chopped fresh parsley leaves,
optional

1 Combine the dried mushrooms in a saucepan with 5
cups water; bring to a boil, cover, turn the heat to low,
and simmer for about 10 minutes, or until tender.

2 Meanwhile put the oil into a skillet, turn the heat to
medium-high, and heat for a minute. Add the fresh
mushrooms and cook, stirring occasionally and seasoning with salt and pepper, until they give up their liquid
and begin to brown. When the dried mushrooms are
tender, scoop them from the liquid with a slotted spoon
and add them to the skillet, along with the garlic and
tomatoes. When all the fresh mushrooms are browned
and the tomatoes are juicy, about 3 minutes later, turn
off the heat.

3 Strain the mushroom-cooking liquid through a
cheesecloth-, napkin-, or towel-lined strainer; measure
it and add water or stock to make sure there are at least 4
cups. Rinse the saucepan and return the liquid to it. Add
the mushroom-tomato mixture and heat through; taste
and adjust the seasoning. Garnish with the parsley if
you like, and serve.

WINE Châteauneuf-du-Pape or another sturdy red

SERVE WITH 60-Minute Bread (page 207) or good store-bought
bread

Pasta, Noodles, and Pizza

Pasta, Risotto Style

Why not cook pasta as you do risotto? That is, add broth a bit at a time and stir frequently, with the goal being a creamy, quickly made pasta (no waiting for the requisite gallon of water to boil!) that requires only marginally more attention than the standard variety. The concept is simple, it makes sense—pasta, like Arborio and other rices used for risotto, is plenty starchy enough—and it just takes the use of good stock and a vegetable to make the dish delicious.

1 pound asparagus

3 tablespoons butter or extra virgin olive oil

1 medium onion, chopped

1 pound penne, gemelli, or other cut pasta

6 to 8 cups good beef or chicken stock, heated

Salt and freshly ground black pepper

Freshly grated Parmigiano-Reggiano, optional

1 Break the woody ends from the asparagus and peel the stalks if necessary. (If you use thin asparagus you won't have to peel them at all; thicker asparagus should be peeled from the bottom of the flower to the end of the stalk.) Break or cut off the flower ends and cut the stems into ½-inch sections (it looks a little nicer if you cut the stems on a diagonal, but this is hardly essential).

2 Put 1½ tablespoons butter or oil in a deep 10- or 12-inch skillet or a broad saucepan and turn the heat to medium-high. When the butter melts, add the onion and cook, stirring occasionally, until softened and beginning to brown, 3 to 5 minutes. Add the pasta and cook, stirring occasionally, until it begins to brown, about 5 minutes more.

3 Add a ladleful of stock. As the stock is absorbed and the pasta swells, add more stock and continue to stir once in a while, until the pasta is beginning to become tender,

WINE Anything from strong, sturdy, high-class red, like super-Tuscan, good Bordeaux, or California Meritage, to Beaujolais, Chianti, or Côtes du Rhône wine

SERVE WITH Made with asparagus, Glazed Carrots (page 201). Made with carrots, Steamed Broccoli (or Other Vegetable) (page 203). Simple Green Salad (page 196) goes well with both versions. (This pasta can also serve as a side dish if you like, and would be perfect next to a breaded sautéed chicken cutlet, for example.)

about 5 minutes. Add the asparagus stalks and continue to add stock as needed, until the pasta is just about done, another 5 minutes or so.

4 Add the asparagus tips and a little more stock, stirring until the tips are crisp-tender, the pasta is cooked to your liking, and the mixture is moist but not soupy (add a little more stock if necessary). Stir in the remaining 1½ tablespoons butter or oil and the cheese and serve.

Keys To SUCCESS

YOU MUST USE cut pasta here, because long pasta is far too unwieldy for this treatment.

IF YOU'RE USING canned stock and have a little time, heat it with an onion, a carrot, and a garlic clove before beginning to add it to the pasta. And don't salt the dish until you're done cooking; canned stock can be overly salty.

With MINIMAL Effort

| Substitute peeled carrots, cut into small chunks, for the asparagus; they add vivid color and a marked sweetness. Or experiment with other vegetables.

| Any sharp grated cheese will fill in well for the Parmigiano-Reggiano, especially Pecorino Romano.

Pasta alla Gricia

TIME: 30 minutes

MAKES: 3 main-course to 6 first-course servings

There is an important and splendid group of pasta recipes that is associated with Rome and the area around it; all the variations begin with bits of cured meat cooked until crisp. Around these delightfully crispy bits—and, of course, their rendered fat—are built a number of difference sauces of increasing complexity. The first contains no more than meat and grated cheese and is called pasta alla gricia; the second, in which eggs are added, is the well-known pasta (usually spaghetti) carbonara, one of the first authentic nontomato pasta dishes to become popular in the United States, about thirty years ago; and the third is pasta all' Amatriciana, which adds the sweetness of cooked onions and the acidity of tomatoes.

2 tablespoons extra virgin olive oil

½ cup minced guanciale, pancetta, or bacon (about ¼ pound)

Salt

1 pound linguine or another long pasta

½ cup grated Pecorino Romano, or more to taste

Freshly ground black pepper

1 Begin heating water for the pasta. In a small saucepan, combine the oil and meat and turn the heat to medium. Cook, stirring occasionally, until the meat is nicely browned, about 10 minutes. Turn off the heat.

2 Salt the boiling pasta water and cook the pasta until it is tender but not mushy. Before draining the pasta, remove about a cup of the cooking water and reserve it.

3 Toss the drained pasta with the meat and its juices; stir in the cheese. If the mixture is dry, add a little of the pasta cooking water (or a little olive oil). Toss in lots of black pepper and serve.

WINE Crisp white, like Pinot Grigio or even Frascati, with the Pasta alla Gricia and Spaghetti Carbonara; Chianti or another light red with Pasta all' Amatriciana

SERVE WITH 60-Minute Bread (page 207) or good store-bought bread; Simple Green Salad (page 196)

COOKBOOKS AND ARTICLES about Italian cooking insist that the "genuine" meat for these recipes is pancetta—salted, cured, and rolled pork belly. Pancetta is available in almost any decent Italian deli and in many specialty stores, but for those of us who cannot obtain pancetta, bacon—which is also pork belly, but cured and smoked—is an adequate substitute. (In fact, the first choice for these dishes is guanciale, salted and cured pig jowl; but that's hard to find.)

SIMILARLY, Pecorino Romano is "essential" to pasta alla gricia, Parmigiano-Reggiano is the most commonly used cheese in carbonara, and the Amatriciana-style sauce is at home with either. But, again, you can choose whatever you like—no one is looking.

Spaghetti Carbonara: Steps 1 and 2 are the same. While the pasta is cooking, warm a large bowl and beat 3 eggs in it. Stir in about ½ cup freshly grated Parmigiano-Reggiano and the pancetta and its juices. When the pasta is done, drain it and toss with the egg mixture. If the mixture is dry (unlikely), add a little reserved cooking water. Add plenty of black pepper and some more cheese and serve.

Pasta all' Amatriciana: Step 1 is the same. Remove the pancetta with a slotted spoon and, in the juices left behind, sauté a sliced, medium onion over medium heat, stirring occasionally, until well softened, about 10 minutes. Turn off the heat and let the mixture cool a bit. Stir in 2 cups chopped tomatoes (canned are fine; drain them first) and turn the heat back to medium. Cook the sauce, stirring occasionally, while you cook the pasta. When the pasta is done, drain it and toss it with the tomato sauce, the reserved pancetta, and at least ½ cup freshly grated Pecorino Romano or Parmigiano-Reggiano cheese.

Pasta with Anchovies and Arugula

A quick way to add great flavor to many simple dinner dishes is already sitting in your pantry or cupboard: It's a can of anchovies. Anchovies are among the original convenience foods and contribute an intense shot of complex brininess that is more like Parmigiano-Reggiano than like canned tuna. Use them, along with garlic, as the base for a bold tomato sauce (page 40), or combine them, as I do here, with greens, garlic, oil, and chiles for a white sauce that packs a punch.

TIME: 30 minutes

MAKES: 3 main-course to 6 first-course servings

4 tablespoons extra virgin olive oil

4 large garlic cloves, peeled and slivered

8 anchovy fillets, or more to taste, with some of their oil

2 cups trimmed arugula, washed, dried, and chopped

Salt

1 pound linguine or other long pasta

Freshly ground black pepper

½ teaspoon or more crushed red pepper flakes

1 Begin heating water for the pasta. Put 2 tablespoons of the oil into a deep skillet, turn the heat to medium, and heat for a minute. Add the garlic and anchovies. When the garlic sizzles and the anchovies break up, turn the heat to the minimum.

2 Salt the boiling pasta water and cook the pasta until it is tender but not mushy. Reserve 1 cup of the cooking liquid and drain. Add the pasta and the arugula to the skillet, along with enough of the reserved cooking water to make a sauce; turn the heat to medium and stir for a minute. Add salt and pepper to taste, plus a pinch or more of the red pepper flakes.

3 Turn into a bowl, toss with the remaining 2 tablespoons oil, and serve.

WINE White and very crisp, like Muscadet or Pinot Grigio; inexpensive Chardonnay would also be good

SERVE WITH Roasted Peppers (page 195); 60-Minute Bread (page 207) or good store-bought bread

ANCHOVIES come in three forms: canned, paste, and salted. Canned are most familiar, and they are a nearly ideal convenience food. It's worth pointing out that you want to buy those packed in olive oil, never soy or cottonseed oil; the ingredients should read "anchovies, olive oil, salt"—no more. Anchovy paste is marginally more convenient. But it's more than twice as expensive by weight as canned anchovies and it often contains cream, butter, preservatives, and other unnecessary ingredients. Salted anchovies, which are sold in bulk in Italian markets from a large can or bucket, are delicious, but a hassle: Before using them, you must rinse them and peel each fillet off the skeleton.

Greens with Anchovies, Pine Nuts, and Raisins: To make this into a nonpasta vegetable dish, follow step 1 as described, then stir in ½ cup each of raisins and pine nuts. Cook for a minute, then add 4 cups of any washed and chopped bitter greens—spinach, arugula, or kale, for example—with about ½ cup water. Cover and cook until the greens are tender, from 5 minutes for spinach or arugula to as long as 20 for kale. Taste and adjust the seasoning if necessary.

Pasta with Cauliflower

Pasta with stewed vegetables—I most often choose cauliflower, but there are many other options—is the one-pot meal I turn to most often when I'm desperate to get something quick, healthy, and filling on the table. It begins with poaching cauliflower, then uses the same water to cook the pasta. The cauliflower and pasta ultimately finish cooking in a mix of extra virgin olive oil, garlic, bread crumbs, and some of the reserved cooking water. The fundamental procedures are easy, and build a wonderfully flavorful dish with just a few ingredients.

1 head cauliflower (about 1 pound)

Salt

¼ cup extra virgin olive oil

1 tablespoon minced garlic

1 cup coarse bread crumbs

1 pound penne, ziti, or other cut pasta

Freshly ground black pepper

1 Bring a large pot of water to a boil. Trim the cauliflower and divide it into florets. Salt the water, add the cauliflower, and cook until the cauliflower is tender but not mushy. Remove the cauliflower and set it aside; when it is cool enough to handle, chop it roughly into small pieces.

2 Combine the oil and garlic in a large, deep skillet over medium-low heat and cook, stirring occasionally, until the garlic is golden, about 5 minutes. Meanwhile, cook the pasta in the same water that you used for the cauliflower.

3 When the garlic is golden, add the cauliflower and bread crumbs to the skillet and turn the heat to medium. Cook, stirring occasionally. When the pasta is just about done—it should be 2 or 3 minutes shy of being the way you like it—drain it, reserving about a cup of the cooking liquid.

4 Add the pasta to the skillet with the cauliflower and toss with a large spoon until well combined. Add salt and pepper to taste, along with some of the pasta water to keep the mixture from drying out. When the mixture is hot and the pasta tender and nicely glazed, serve.

WINE Chianti, Beaujolais, or another light red

SERVE WITH Simple Green Salad (page 196)

BE CAREFUL with the garlic—it should not brown in the oil but just begin to color.

MAKE SURE YOU drain the pasta well short of the doneness stage, because you want to spend 3 to 4 minutes tossing it in the olive oil along with some of the cooking water, without it becoming too soft.

With MINIMAL Effort

| Substitute broccoli, broccoli raab, or kale for the cauliflower.

| Substitute freshly grated Parmigiano-Reggiano for the bread crumbs.

| Add 3 or 4 anchovy fillets, with their oil, to the skillet along with the garlic.

| Add some crumbled sausage meat or chopped shrimp to the garlic mixture along with the bread crumbs.

| Garnish with chopped parsley or basil.

Pasta with Fresh Herbs

TIME: 30 minutes
MAKES: 3 main-course to 6 first-course servings

All winter, I dream of the time when there are so many fresh herbs that it seems imperative to use them at almost every meal. One of my favorite ways to take advantage of this abundance is to mix large quantities of herbs with pasta and a simple base of olive oil and garlic. In winter, a dish like this would not only seem exotic but would also cost a small fortune. In summer, however, it is an inexpensive no-brainer.

¼ cup extra virgin olive oil, or more to taste

1 teaspoon minced garlic

1 cup or more mixed herbs, such as parsley, dill, chervil, basil, tarragon, sage, thyme, oregano, marjoram, or mint (leaves and thin stems only)

1 tablespoon butter, optional

Salt

1 pound linguine or other long pasta

Freshly ground black pepper

1   Begin heating a large pot of water for the pasta. Meanwhile, combine the oil and garlic in a small saucepan and turn the heat to medium-low. Cook gently, just until the garlic beings to color, then remove from the heat. Meanwhile, wash and mince the herbs. Place them in a bowl large enough to hold the pasta. Cut the butter into bits, if you're using it, and add it to the bowl.

2   Salt the boiling pasta water and cook the pasta until tender but not mushy. Reserve ½ cup of the pasta cooking water, then drain the pasta and toss with the herbs and reserved oil-garlic mixture. Add a little more olive oil or some of the pasta water if you did not use butter and the mixture seems dry. Season with salt and pepper and serve.

WINE   A chilled, dry rosé from Provence or elsewhere; a crisp, light white; or fruity, light red

SERVE WITH   Tomato Salad with Basil (page 198); 60-Minute Bread (page 207) or good store-bought bread

THE MOST RELIABLE HERBS are parsley or basil, because each can be used in large quantities without overwhelming the flavor of the dish, and both are widely available. Chervil, a delicious and underrated herb that tends to be expensive and even difficult to find because it is so fragile, is great as a supporting character here, as are dill, marjoram, mint, and oregano. More powerful herbs, including thyme, sage, tarragon, and rosemary, should be used more sparingly; a teaspoon—or a tablespoon in the case of sage—is plenty.

I LIKE TO ADD a little butter to the sauce, which adds both creaminess and flavor, but you can certainly finish the dish with a bit of olive oil instead, or even with some of the water in which the pasta cooked.

Some interesting herb combinations include

½ cup each of parsley and basil, ¼ cup dill, and 1 teaspoon each of thyme and tarragon

⅓ cup each of parsley, chervil, and marjoram, with a few needles of rosemary

½ cup marjoram, ¼ cup dill, 1 teaspoon of thyme or tarragon

Pasta with Parsley Sauce

Parsley is the most reliable and under-rated herb in the western culinary world. Although we've come a long way from the days when its major role was as a decorative sprig on the side of a plate, we still don't use parsley in the kinds of quantities we could. Here, it is cooked like a vegetable—like spinach, really—to create a delicious, fresh-tasting pasta sauce, one that provides blessed relief in the winter and can become a staple in the summer.

2 tablespoons butter or extra virgin olive oil

¼ cup minced shallot or onion

2 or 3 bunches parsley, (about 1 pound), stemmed, washed, and dried

1 cup heavy cream or half-and-half

Salt

1 pound cut pasta, such as ziti or penne

Freshly ground black pepper

Freshly grated Parmigiano-Reggiano

1 Begin heating a large pot of water for the pasta. Put the butter or oil in a deep skillet and turn the heat to medium. When the butter melts, or the oil is hot, add the shallot or onion and cook, stirring occasionally, until softened, 3 to 5 minutes. Add the parsley and cook, stirring, for about a minute. Add the cream and turn the heat to low.

2 Salt the pasta water and cook the pasta until it is tender but not mushy. Season the parsley mixture with salt and pepper. Drain the pasta, toss it with the parsley mixture and some grated cheese, and serve.

WINE Good Chardonnay or white Burgundy, preferably (real) Chablis

SERVE WITH 60-Minute Bread (page 207) or good store-bought bread

PARSLEY'S THICK STEMS must be removed (you can use them for stock) and the leaves carefully washed. They should be dried as well, at least somewhat, so a salad spinner is the best tool for this task.

Pasta with Spinach Sauce: Use about 10 ounces spinach, stemmed, washed, and chopped, in place of the parsley.

Creamed Parsley: Serve this "sauce" as a vegetable dish, without the pasta. It will look like creamed spinach, but taste much different.

Pasta with Green Beans, Potatoes, and Pesto

Trenette with Pesto

Pesto has become a staple, especially in late summer when basil is at its best. But pasta with pesto does have its limits; it's simply not substantial enough to serve as a main course. The Genoese, originators of pesto, figured this out centuries ago, when they created trenette with pesto. Trenette is a pasta almost identical to linguine, and trenette with pesto (trenette is always served with pesto) often contains chunks of potatoes and green beans, which make it more complex, more filling, and more interesting than plain pasta with pesto. Recreating this classic dish is straightforward and easy.

2 cups basil leaves

2 garlic cloves, peeled

Salt

½ cup grated Pecorino Romano or other hard sheep's-milk cheese or Parmigiano-Reggiano

½ cup extra virgin olive oil, or more to taste

2 tablespoons pine nuts

2 medium potatoes (about ½ pound), peeled and cut into ½-inch cubes

1 pound trenette or linguine

½ pound green beans, trimmed and cut into 1-inch lengths

1 Begin heating a large pot of water for the potatoes and pasta. Combine the basil, garlic, salt to taste, and cheese in a blender or food processor; pulse until roughly chopped. Add ½ cup oil in a steady stream, and continue to blend until the mixture is fairly creamy, adding a little more oil or some water, if necessary. Add the pine nuts, and pulse a few times to chop them into the sauce.

2 Salt the boiling water. Add the potatoes and stir; cook for 3 minutes, then add the pasta, and cook as usual, stirring frequently, about 10 minutes in all. When the pasta is about half done—the strands will bend but are not yet tender—add the green beans.

3 When the pasta is done, the potatoes and beans should be tender. Drain the pasta and vegetables, toss with pesto and more salt or olive oil, if you like, and serve.

WINE Beaujolais, Chianti, or another light, fruity red

SERVE WITH Assuming it's summer, Raw Beet Salad (page 194) or Simple Green Salad (page 196)

IF YOU START the potatoes and pasta simultaneously, then add the green beans about halfway through cooking, they will all be finished at the same time and can be drained and tossed with the sauce in a snap. This technique may sound imprecise, but it works.

TO PREVENT the potatoes from falling apart, use a waxy variety, such as Red Bliss, or at least a not-especially-starchy all-purpose variety, like Yukon gold.

ANY KIND of green beans will work, although thinner beans, like delicate, flavorful haricots verts, should be added a minute or two later than common green beans.

| Make the pesto without the cheese or nuts if you like.

| Make the dish extra-rich by stirring in a bit of softened butter instead of olive oil at the end.

Linguine with Tomato-Anchovy Sauce

TIME: 30 minutes

MAKES: 3 main-course to 6 first-course servings

Few things are simpler than a quick tomato sauce over pasta, but as an unending diet it can become some-what tiresome. Here it's completely jazzed by the addition of a hefty amount of garlic and a few anchovies. The transformation is as easy as it is remarkable.

2 tablespoons extra virgin olive oil

1 teaspoon minced garlic

4 to 6 anchovy fillets, with some of their oil

One 28-ounce can tomatoes, crushed or chopped and drained of their juice

1 pound linguine

Salt and freshly ground black pepper

1 Begin heating a large pot of water for the pasta. Pour the oil in a deep skillet, turn the heat to medium, and heat for a minute. Add the garlic and the anchovies. When the garlic sizzles and the anchovies break up, add the tomatoes.

2 Turn the heat to medium-high and bring to a boil. Cook, stirring occasionally, until the mixture becomes saucy, about 15 minutes.

3 Salt the pasta water and cook the pasta until it is tender but not mushy. Season the sauce with salt and pepper to taste. Drain the pasta, toss it with the sauce, and serve.

WINE Chianti or any spirited red

SERVE WITH 60-Minute Bread (page 207) or good store-bought bread

CANNED ANCHOVIES—packed in olive oil—are the easiest to use here. Salted anchovies, if you have them, are fine also, but you must mince them first (after cleaning them, of course, which you do under running water, stripping the meat from the skeleton).

| This dish doesn't need cheese; but if you're going to use it, Pecorino Romano is best.

| You can, of course, omit the anchovies and make a milder sauce. To tame it even further, substitute ½ cup chopped onion for the garlic. If you want to go in the other direction, add a sprinkling of crushed red pepper flakes, or cook a dried chile or two with the garlic.

| Garnish with chopped parsley or basil if you like.

Pasta with Clams and Tomatoes

TIME: 30 to 40 minutes

MAKES: 3 main-course to 6 first-course servings

Every time I think I have come up with the ultimate pasta and clam dish, someone shows me a better one. This is a technique I learned in Liguria—the Italian Riviera—in which all of the clam liquid is used as part of the sauce, but without much effort. The result is delicious pasta in a rich, thick sauce—along with a pile of clams.

4 tablespoons extra virgin olive oil

36 to 48 littleneck clams, well-washed

1 tablespoon minced garlic

Salt

1 pound linguine or other long pasta

2 or 3 plum tomatoes, cored and chopped

Freshly ground black pepper

Chopped parsley

1 Begin heating a large pot of water for the pasta. Pour 2 tablespoons of the oil into a large, deep skillet, turn the heat to high, and heat for a minute. Add the clams, reduce the heat to medium-high, give the pan a shake, and cover. Continue to cook the clams, shaking the pan occasionally, until they begin to open, about 5 minutes. Add the garlic and cook until most of the clams are open.

2 Salt the boiling pasta water and cook the pasta. When it is nearly tender, remove a cup of its cooking water and drain. When the clams are ready, add the pasta and the tomatoes to the skillet and cook, tossing frequently, until the pasta is tender and hot; add some of the pasta-cooking water if the mixture is too dry.

3 Add the remaining 2 tablespoons oil and taste and adjust the seasoning if necessary; garnish with the parsley and serve.

WINE Pinot Grigio, Orvieto, Vernaccia, or another crisp Italian white

SERVE WITH 60-Minute bread (page 207) or good store-bought bread; Simple Green Salad (page 196)

STOP COOKING THE PASTA while it is still quite stiff, but be sure to reserve a little of its cooking water before you drain it. It will finish cooking in the clam juices, along with a little of the reserved water.

USE THE SMALLEST CLAMS you can find; cockles are fine, too. Figure eight to twelve littlenecks or twenty-four cockles per person. Wash and scrub the clamshells very well, as they will cook in the sauce and any unremoved sand will find its way into your mouth. Discard any open or cracked clams before cooking; those that remain shut after cooking may be opened with a knife.

White Pasta with Clams: Substitute about ¾ cup dry white wine for the tomatoes, adding it to the clams about 1 minute before the pasta.

Stir-Fried Coconut Noodles

TIME: 45 minutes
MAKES: 4 servings

Rice noodles have no equivalent in European cooking. Made from rice powder and almost always sold dried, they are nearly as fast-cooking as fresh wheat noodles. Regardless of their name (rice stick, rice vermicelli, oriental-style noodle, and so on), rice noodles are easily recognized by their gray-white, translucent appearance, and by the fact that because of their somewhat irregular shapes they are never packed in as orderly a fashion as wheat noodles. (They are quite long and are packaged folded up over themselves.) Two thicknesses are common: very thin and fettuccinelike; here you want the latter.

¾ pound fettucine-style rice noodles

3 tablespoons grapeseed, corn, or other light oil

1 pound minced or ground boneless pork or chicken

1 yellow or red bell pepper, stemmed, seeded, and minced

1 eggplant (about ½ pound), cut into ½-inch cubes

1 tablespoon minced garlic

One 12- to 14-ounce can (about 1½ cups) unsweetened coconut milk

Nam pla (fish sauce), soy sauce, or salt

Freshly ground black pepper

Minced cilantro

1 Soak the noodles in very hot water to cover until you're ready to add them to the stir-fry.

2 Meanwhile, pour 1 tablespoon of the oil into a large skillet or wok, turn the heat to high, and heat for a minute. Add the meat and cook, stirring occasionally, until it browns and loses its raw look, about 5 minutes. Remove with a slotted spoon and set aside.

3 Add another 1 tablespoon oil to the skillet, followed by the bell pepper and eggplant. Cook over medium-high heat, stirring occasionally, until the pepper and eggplant are browned and tender, about 10 minutes. Remove with a slotted spoon and combine with the meat.

4 Add the remaining 1 tablespoon oil, followed immediately by the garlic and cook for about 30 seconds. Add the coconut milk. Cook over medium-high heat, stirring

WINE Beer, Pinot Blanc, not-too-sweet Gewürztraminer, or Riesling

SERVE WITH Green Salad with Soy Vinaigrette (page 197)

and scraping with a wooden spoon, for about a minute. Drain the noodles and add along with the meat and vegetables. Cook until the noodles absorb most of the coconut milk, about 3 minutes.

5 Season with nam pla, soy sauce, or salt to taste, then add plenty of black pepper. Garnish with cilantro and serve.

RICE NOODLES need only be soaked in hot water for a few minutes to become tender. Some cooking is desirable after that, but stir-frying is sufficient.

YOU CAN SUBSTITUTE Italian linguine or spaghetti for the rice noodles. Although the texture will not be the same, the dish will still be good. Boil the noodles nearly to doneness in the normal fashion, then rinse before proceeding.

USE SOY SAUCE if you do not have fish sauce (nam pla), the Thai liquid seasoning that is available at all Asian markets.

TO MAKE YOUR OWN coconut milk, combine 2 cups grated unsweetened coconut and 2 cups boiling water in a blender; let cool a bit, then blend, taking care that the hot liquid does not splatter, carefully. Strain and discard solids.

With MINIMAL Effort

Meatless Coconut Noodles: Substitute ½ pound chopped shrimp or other shellfish for the pork or chicken; or omit the meat if you like, with no substitutions.

Substitute partially cooked broccoli florets, broken into small pieces, for the eggplant.

Add crushed red pepper flakes or Tabasco sauce to taste.

Stir-Fried Noodles with Shrimp

Here's another use for rice noodles. This one is akin to the popular (in the U.S. at least) Thai restaurant dish known as pad Thai. There are a lot of ingredients here, but most of them keep well in your pantry, and substituting is easy.

6 dried black (shiitake) mushrooms (or use fresh shiitakes, trimmed of their stems and sliced)

12 ounces thin rice noodles ("vermicelli" or "rice stick")

2 tablespoons peanut or grapeseed, corn, or other light oil

1 tablespoon slivered or minced garlic

12 ounces shrimp, peeled (deveined if you like) and cut into bite-size pieces

½ teaspoon Asian chile paste or crushed red pepper flakes, or to taste

2 eggs, lightly beaten

3 tablespoons soy sauce, or to taste

2 teaspoons sugar

Stock (or water or mushroom-soaking liquid) as needed

Salt, optional

1 cup bean sprouts, optional

½ cup washed, dried, and torn basil leaves, preferably Thai basil, optional

1 Put the dried mushrooms in a small bowl and cover them with boiling water (don't soak fresh mushrooms). Put the noodles in a large bowl and cover them with hot water. Prepare the other ingredients. When the mushrooms are soft, about 10 minutes later, drain, reserving their soaking liquid; trim and slice them.

2 Put the oil in a large nonstick skillet and turn the heat to high. Add the garlic and stir; add the shrimp and cook, stirring occasionally, for about a minute. Stir in the chile paste.

3 Drain the noodles and add to the skillet. Cook, stirring occasionally, for about a minute. Make a well in the center of the noodles and pour the eggs into this well. Scramble, gradually integrating the egg with the noo-

WINE Beer or not-too-dry Gewürztraminer or Riesling
SERVE WITH Green Salad with Soy Vinaigrette (page 197)

dles; this will take less than a minute. Stir in the soy sauce and sugar. If the noodles are "clumpy," add about ½ cup of liquid to allow them to separate and become saucy (use more liquid if necessary, but do not make the mixture soupy). Add salt to taste, then stir in the bean sprouts and basil, if using. Turn off the heat and serve.

Keys To SUCCESS

See page 45 for techniques for preparing rice noodles.

See page 45 for techniques for preparing rice noodles.

With MINIMAL Effort

Stir-Fried Rice Noodles with Chicken or Pork: For the shrimp, substitute finely chopped or ground chicken or pork.

| Use finely chopped cabbage in place of the bean sprouts.

| For the soy sauce, substitute nam pla (Thai fish sauce) or hoisin sauce.

Fresh Chinese Noodles with Brown Sauce

TIME: 20 to 30 minutes
MAKES: 4 servings

You can find fresh Chinese- (and Japanese-) style noodles in most supermarkets these days. They're a great convenience food, and for some reason seem more successful than prepackaged "fresh" Italian noodles. Here, they're briefly cooked and then combined with a stir-fried mixture of pork, vegetables, and Chinese sauces; it's very much a Chinese restaurant dish.

½ to ¾ pound ground pork

1 cup minced scallions

1 tablespoon peeled and minced ginger

1 tablespoon minced garlic

1 cup chicken stock or water

2 tablespoons ground bean sauce

2 tablespoon hoisin sauce

1 tablespoon soy sauce

1 pound fresh egg or wheat noodles (see above)

1 tablespoon toasted sesame oil

1 Begin heating a large pot of water for the noodles. Meanwhile, put a large skillet over medium-high heat. Add the pork, crumbling it to bits as you add it and stirring to break up any clumps. Add ½ cup scallions, along with the ginger and garlic, and stir. Add the stock or water; stir in the bean, hoisin, and soy sauces and cook, stirring occasionally, until thick, about 5 minutes. Reduce the heat and keep warm.

2 Cook the noodles, stirring, until tender, 3 to 5 minutes. Drain and dress with the sauce. Garnish with the remaining ½ cup scallions, drizzle the sesame oil over all, and serve.

WINE Beer or not-too-dry Gewürztraminer or Riesling

SERVE WITH Green Salad with Soy Vinaigrette (page 197), Sautéed Shiitake Mushrooms (page 202), and/or Steamed Broccoli (or Other Vegetable) (page 203), drizzled with a little soy sauce

BOTH GROUND BEAN SAUCE and hoisin sauce can be found in supermarkets, but you can usually find a better selection (and higher quality versions) in Chinese markets. Usually, the fewer ingredients they contain, the better they are. If you can't find ground bean sauce, just use a little more hoisin.

Fresh Chinese Noodles with Chicken, or Meatless Fresh Chinese Noodles: Substitute ground chicken or turkey for the pork: or eliminate the meat entirely, sautéing the scallions, ginger, and garlic in a couple of tablespoons of peanut oil.

| Toss the noodles with a cup of bean sprouts or lightly stir-fried snow peas before dressing.

The Minimalist's Pizzas

Pizza is easy, even when you make the dough yourself. And although we have practically been force-fed pizza with cooked tomato sauce, pizza is even easier, and equally satisfying, when topped with raw ingredients. It may be that there are more possible combinations of pizza toppings than moves in chess or atoms in the universe; in any case, there are a lot. Simple combinations are best; too many ingredients merely serve to muddy the flavors.

What the following pizzas have in common is their uncooked toppings; once you get the hang of it, you'll find it easy enough to improvise with both raw and cooked ingredients.

TIME: 1 hour or more, largely unattended
MAKES: 1 large or 2 or more smaller pies

Pizza Dough

3 cups all-purpose or bread flour, plus more as needed

2 teaspoons instant yeast, such as SAF

2 teaspoons coarse kosher or sea salt, plus extra for sprinkling

2 tablespoons extra virgin olive oil

1 Combine the flour, yeast, and salt in the container of a food processor. Turn the machine on and add 1 cup cold water and the oil through the feed tube.

2 Process for about 30 seconds, adding up to ¼ cup more water, a little at a time, until the mixture forms a ball and is slightly sticky to the touch. If it is dry, add another 1 to 2 tablespoons water and process for another 10 seconds. (In the unlikely event that the mixture is too sticky, add flour, a tablespoon at a time.)

3 Turn the dough onto a floured work surface and knead by hand for a few seconds to form a smooth, round dough ball. Put the dough in a bowl and cover with plastic wrap; let rise until the dough doubles in size, 1 to 2 hours. (Or you can let the dough rise more slowly, in the refrigerator, for up to 6 or 8 hours.) Proceed to step 4, or wrap the dough tightly in plastic wrap and freeze for up to a month. (Defrost in a covered bowl in the refrigerator or at room temperature.)

4 When the dough is ready, form it into a ball and divide it into two or more pieces if you like; roll each piece into a round ball. Place each ball on lightly floured surface, sprinkle with a little flour, and cover with plastic wrap or a towel. Let rest until they puff slightly, about 20 minutes. Proceed with any recipe below.

WINE Chianti or another rough red is usually the best bet.
SERVE WITH Roasted Peppers (page 195), Simple Green Salad (page 196), and/or Tomato Salad with Basil (page 198)

THERE ARE THREE WAYS to obtain pizza dough: My favorite is making it in the food processor, which does a quick, efficient job. You can also make dough by hand; and although it's hardly what you'd call convenient it isn't difficult. Finally, you can buy dough, either in the supermarket (usually in the freezer; use white bread dough if pizza dough isn't available) or, better still, from the local pizza shop (just ask; you'll usually be accommodated). But it's easier to make a batch in the food processor than to go to the store—really.

I SPECIFY SAF or other instant yeast in the recipe; this is yeast that can be mixed, dry, with the flour—it's fuss-free, keeps forever in the fridge, and is sold in every supermarket.

BE SURE TO ALLOW the dough to relax, stretching it a little bit at a time, when you're ready to roll it out; pressing the dough onto an oiled baking sheet is the easiest way to get this done. And bear in mind that it's easier to handle small pies than large ones.

YOU CAN BAKE the pies or grill them. An oven lined with a baking stone (or several uncoated quarry tiles) is ideal, but it requires a peel (a flat sheet of wood or metal with a long handle) to move the pizza about. A baking sheet, with or without a lip, is much easier, because you can press the dough right onto its surface. Since you use olive oil to prevent sticking, the process is a snap.

GENERALLY, TOPPINGS should never be too wet, or the dough will become soggy. In practice, this means fresh tomatoes should have some of their juice squeezed out and be thinly sliced, and preferably salted for a little while, before using; the same holds true for other moist vegetables like zucchini.

SOME PEOPLE THINK all pizzas must have cheese in order to bind the other ingredients, but this is ridiculously limiting. What you put on a pizza is entirely up to you—if the kitchen sink is your idea of fun, go right ahead.

Pizza with Tomatoes, Onions, and Olives

TIME: 30 to 45 minutes
(with premade dough)

Pizza Dough (page 50)

4 or 5 ripe tomatoes

Coarse salt

1 medium red onion or 4 shallots, chopped

20 black olives, kalamata or oil-cured, pitted and chopped

Extra virgin olive oil as needed

1 FOR GRILLED PIZZA, start a medium-hot charcoal or wood fire, or preheat a gas grill to the maximum. Roll or lightly press each dough ball into a flat round, lightly flouring the work surface and the dough as necessary (do not use more flour than you need to). Let the rounds sit for a few minutes, then roll or pat out the dough, as thinly as you like, turning occasionally and sprinkling the top with flour as necessary.

FOR BAKED PIZZA, preheat the oven to 500° F. Oil one or more baking sheets, then press each dough ball into a flat round directly on the oiled sheet(s). Then pat out the dough, as thinly as you like, oiling your hands if necessary. If your oven is equipped with a baking stone, roll or pat out the dough as for grilled pizza, above.

2 Core the tomatoes (cut a cone-shaped wedge out of the stem end), then cut them in half horizontally. Gently squeeze out the liquid and shake out most of the seeds, then slice the tomatoes as thinly as possible. Salt them lightly and let them sit for at least 10 minutes, then drain off any excess liquid.

3 TO GRILL THE PIZZA, slide it directly onto the grill. Cook until brown grill marks appear, about 3 to 5 minutes, depending on your grill heat. Turn with a spatula or tongs, top with the tomatoes, onions, and olives, and drizzle with olive oil. Cover the grill and cook until the bottom is crisp and brown and the tomatoes are hot, just a few more minutes.

TO BAKE THE PIZZA, top with tomatoes, onions, olives, and a little olive oil, and slide the baking sheet into the oven (or the pizza itself onto the stone), and bake for about 15 minutes, depending on the oven heat, or until nicely browned.

Pizza with Zucchini and Sausage

TIME: 40 to 50 minutes
(with premade dough)

Pizza Dough (page 50)

Olive oil as needed

4 small or 2 large zucchini, about 1 pound

Coarse salt

2 or 3 sweet Italian sausages, the meat removed from the casing and crumbled

2 teaspoons minced garlic

1 FOR GRILLED PIZZA, start a medium-hot charcoal or wood fire, or preheat a gas grill to the maximum. Roll or lightly press each dough ball into a flat round, lightly flouring the work surface and the dough as necessary (do not use more flour than you need to). Let the rounds sit for a few minutes, then roll or pat out the dough, as thinly as you like, turning occasionally and sprinkling the top with flour as necessary.

FOR BAKED PIZZA, preheat the oven to 500° F. Oil one or more baking sheets, then press each dough ball into a flat round directly on the oiled sheet(s). Pat out the dough, as thinly as you like, oiling your hands if necessary. If your oven is equipped with a baking stone, roll or pat out the dough as for grilled pizza, above.

2 Thinly slice the zucchini. Salt the slices lightly and let them sit for at least 20 minutes, then drain off any accumulated liquid.

3 TO GRILL THE PIZZA, slide it directly onto the grill. Cook until brown grill marks appear, about 3 to 5 minutes, depending on your grill heat. Turn with a spatula or tongs, then top with the zucchini, sausage, and garlic. Cover the grill and cook until the bottom is crisp and brown and the sausage cooked through, 5 to 10 minutes.

TO BAKE THE PIZZA, top with the zucchini, sausage, and garlic and slide the baking sheet into the oven (or the pizza itself onto the stone), and bake for about 15 minutes, depending on the oven heat, or until nicely browned.

Pizza with Green Tomatoes

TIME: 40 to 50 minutes
(with premade dough)

Pizza Dough (page 50)

Olive oil as needed

2 large or 4 small green tomatoes

1 cup freshly grated Parmigiano-
   Reggiano

½ cup coarsely chopped or torn basil

1 FOR GRILLED PIZZA, start a medium-hot charcoal or wood fire, or preheat a gas grill to the maximum. Roll or lightly press each dough ball into a flat round, lightly flouring the work surface and the dough as necessary (do not use more flour than you need to). Let the rounds sit for a few minutes, then roll or pat out the dough, as thinly as you like, turning occasionally and sprinkling the top with flour as necessary.

FOR BAKED PIZZA, preheat the oven to 500° F. Oil one or more baking sheets, then press each dough ball into a flat round directly on the oiled sheet(s). Pat out the dough, as thinly as you like, oiling your hands if necessary. If your oven is equipped with a baking stone, roll or pat out the dough as for grilled pizza, above.

2 Core and thinly slice the tomatoes. Salt the slices lightly and let them sit for at least 20 minutes, then drain off any accumulated liquid.

3 TO GRILL THE PIZZA, slide it directly onto the grill. Cook until brown grill marks appear, about 3 to 5 minutes, depending on your grill heat. Turn with a spatula or tongs, then top with the tomatoes, cheese, and basil. Cover the grill and cook until the bottom is crisp and brown and the top hot, 5 to 10 minutes.

TO BAKE THE PIZZA, top with the tomatoes and cheese, and slide the baking sheet into the oven (or the pizza itself onto the stone), and bake for about 10 minutes, depending on the oven heat, or until nearly done. Sprinkle with the basil and bake until the pizza is done, a few more minutes.

Pizza with Four Cheeses and Basil

TIME: 30 to 40 minutes
(with premade dough

Pizza Dough (page 50)

Olive oil as needed

½ cup shredded or cubed mozzarella cheese

½ cup shredded or cubed Fontina or Taleggio cheese

½ cup freshly grated Pecorino Romano cheese

½ cup freshly grated Parmigiano-Reggiano cheese

½ cup coarsely chopped or torn basil

1 FOR GRILLED PIZZA, start a charcoal or wood fire, or preheat a gas grill to the maximum. Roll or lightly press each dough ball into a flat round, lightly flouring the work surface and the dough as necessary (do not use more flour than you need to). Let the rounds sit for a few minutes, then roll or pat out the dough, as thinly as you like, turning occasionally and sprinkling the top with flour as necessary.

FOR BAKED PIZZA, preheat the oven to 500° F. Oil one or more baking sheets, then press each dough ball into a flat round directly on the oiled sheet(s). Pat out the dough, as thinly as you like, oiling your hands if necessary. If your oven is equipped with a baking stone, roll or pat out the dough as for grilled pizza, above.

3 TO GRILL THE PIZZA, slide it directly onto the grill. Cook until brown grill marks appear, about 3 to 5 minutes, depending on your grill heat. Turn with a spatula or tongs, then top with the cheeses and basil. Cover the grill and cook until the bottom is crisp and brown and the cheeses are melted, 5 to 10 minutes.

TO BAKE THE PIZZA, top with the cheeses and slide the baking sheet into the oven (or the pizza itself onto the stone), and bake for about 10 minutes, or until nearly done. Sprinkle with the basil and finish baking, a few more minutes.

Pizza with Arugula, Corn, and Bacon

Pizza Dough (page 50)

Olive oil as needed

6 cups loosely packed washed, dried, and
shredded arugula

Kernels from 4 ears corn

½ cup minced bacon

1 FOR GRILLED PIZZA, start a charcoal or wood fire, or preheat a gas grill to the maximum. Roll or lightly press each dough ball into a flat round, lightly flouring the work surface and the dough as necessary (do not use more flour than you need to). Let the rounds sit for a few minutes, then roll or pat out the dough, as thinly as you like, turning occasionally and sprinkling the top with flour as necessary.

FOR BAKED PIZZA, preheat the oven to 500° F. Oil one or more baking sheets, then press each dough ball into a flat round directly on the oiled sheet(s). Pat out the dough, as thinly as you like, oiling your hands if necessary. If your oven is equipped with a baking stone, roll or pat out the dough as for grilled pizza, above.

2 TO GRILL THE PIZZA, slide it directly onto the grill. Cook until brown grill marks appear, about 3 to 5 minutes, depending on your grill heat. Turn with a spatula or tongs, then top with the arugula, corn, and bacon. Cover the grill and cook until the bottom is crisp and brown and the bacon cooked through.

TO BAKE THE PIZZA, top with the arugula, corn, and bacon and slide the baking sheet into the oven (or the pizza itself onto the stone), and bake for about 15 minutes, or until nicely browned.

Try these extremely basic (and wonderful) combinations, none of which requires precooking:

White Pizza: Drizzle with about 2 tablespoons olive oil, then sprinkle with coarse salt, about a tablespoon of fresh rosemary leaves (or 1 to 2 teaspoons dried) and, if you like, a bit of minced garlic, chopped onions, or chopped shallots.

Pizza Romano: Drizzle with about 2 tablespoons olive oil, then top with a lot of cracked black pepper and a good cup of freshly grated Pecorino Romano cheese.

Pizza with Parmigiano-Reggiano and Sage: Top with at least a cup of freshly grated Parmigiano-Reggiano cheese, then sprinkle with 20 or 30 coarsely chopped fresh sage leaves.

Pizza with Shallots and Thyme: Drizzle with about 2 tablespoons olive oil, then sprinkle with coarse salt and freshly cracked black pepper, a cup slivered shallots, and about a teaspoon fresh thyme leaves (or a few pinches dried thyme).

Pesto Pizza: Spread with about a cup pesto, or simply a handful or two of basil, along with some garlic and a couple of tablespoons of extra virgin olive oil.

Pizza with Mozzarella: Top with a couple of handfuls of grated mozzarella cheese, some sliced tomatoes, and a lot of chopped basil, along with a sprinkling of salt and pepper and a drizzle of olive oil.

BLACK SKILLET MUSSELS

FENNEL-STEAMED MUSSELS, PROVENCE STYLE

CRABBY CRABCAKES

SOUTHEAST ASIAN SHRIMP AND GRAPEFRUIT SALAD

COLD POACHED SHRIMP WITH MARJORAM "PESTO"

SPANISH-STYLE SHRIMP

SHRIMP COOKED IN LIME JUICE

SHRIMP, ROMAN STYLE

SHRIMP WITH BETTER COCKTAIL SAUCE

SHRIMP IN "BARBECUE" SAUCE

SPICY SHRIMP

SCALLOPS "A LA PLANCHA"

CURRIED SCALLOPS WITH TOMATOES

Shellfish

SCALLOPS WITH ALMONDS

TRIPLE SESAME SALAD WITH SCALLOPS

SQUID IN RED WINE SAUCE

Black Skillet Mussels

TIME: 30 minutes
MAKES: 2 servings

Many years ago in Barcelona, I saw mussels and clams cooked *a la plancha*—on a thick slab of hot metal much like the griddles used by short-order cooks. The technique is common in Spain, and indeed throughout the Mediterranean. Though the mollusks are usually served unadorned, they're filled with their own flavors as well as a certain smokiness contributed by their juices, which burn on the hot surface. This smokiness sometimes makes people think that mussels cooked this way are cooked over wood, but that is not the case, nor is it necessary. San Francisco chef Reed Hearon devised this method of achieving the same results in an ordinary cast-iron skillet, and it works beautifully.

1½ pounds mussels, washed and debearded

Salt and freshly ground black pepper

1 Heat a large cast-iron or heavy steel skillet over high heat for about 5 minutes, or until a few drops of water dance across the surface. Add the mussels to the skillet, in one layer (your pan may fit more or less than 1½ pounds; use as many as will fit comfortably).

2 Cook, shaking the pan occasionally, until the mussels begin to open. The mussels are done when they're all open and their juices have run out and evaporated in the hot pan, probably less than 10 minutes. Sprinkle with salt and pepper and serve immediately, in the pan.

WINE A chilled rosé from southern France or California or a crisp white like Muscadet

SERVE WITH Serve this before or after pasta like Pasta with Anchovies and Arugula (page 30) or Pasta with Cauliflower (page 32); Simple Green Salad (page 196)

FARMED MUSSELS are almost always cleaner than wild mussels and will require no more than a quick rinse and removal of the "beard," the weedy growth attached to the bottom of the shell. Discard any with broken shells, those whose shells remain open after tapping them lightly, and those that seem unusually heavy—chances are they're filled with mud. As long as you do this, any mussels that don't open fully during cooking are still safe to eat; just pry apart their shells with a knife.

THE SKILLET should be hot but not white; when a few drops of water dance across its surface, it's ready.

IT'S BEST TO serve the mussels in the same skillet in which they were cooked. To eat, remove a mussel from the shell and dredge it in the dried juices of the pan.

Black Skillet Clams or Oysters: This dish can be made with hardshell clams—littlenecks, cherrystones, or quahogs—or with oysters. (Softshell clams, or steamers, are too sandy for this treatment.) Make sure to wash the shells of any of these mollusks very well, and discard any whose shells are open or cracked. As with the mussels, they are done when their shells open.

| Gently melt ¼ cup (½ stick) butter in a small saucepan. (If you like, add Tabasco or other hot sauce to taste, along with the juice of a lemon.) Serve the mussels with a small bowl of the butter. To eat, remove a mussel from its shell; dip into the butter, then rub up some of the dried juices from the bottom of the skillet.

| When the mussels begin to open, add 4 crushed garlic cloves to the pan, shaking the pan as above.

Fennel-Steamed Mussels, Provence Style

In a café in southern France more than twenty years ago, I sat in a bistro and timidly prepared to order salade Niçoise. Just then, a huge bowl of steaming, powerfully fragrant mussels was delivered to a man sitting at the table next to me, and I impulsively changed my order. The hot mussels were essentially tossed with fennel and fennel seeds, which I could see, but the licorice bouquet and indeed flavor were far stronger than that combination alone could provide. Later, I realized that there was a secret ingredient: anise liqueur, either Pernod or Ricard. The combination is an alluring one.

2 tablespoons extra virgin olive oil

4 garlic cloves, smashed and peeled

1 fennel bulb (about 1 pound), trimmed and thinly sliced

2 tablespoons fennel seeds

½ cup Pernod or Ricard (or 4 pieces star anise)

1 cup chopped tomatoes (canned are fine; drain them first), optional

1 sprig tarragon, optional

At least 4 pounds large mussels, well washed

1 Pour the oil into a large pot, turn the heat to medium, and heat for a minute. Add the garlic, fennel, fennel seeds, liqueur, tomatoes, and tarragon, if you like. Bring to a boil, cook for about a minute, add the mussels, cover the pot, and turn the heat to high.

2 Cook, shaking the pot occasionally, until the mussels open, 5 to 10 minutes. Use a slotted spoon to remove the mussels and fennel to a serving bowl, then strain any liquid over them and serve.

WINE   White, crisp, and cold—Muscadet, an inexpensive Italian white, or a good Sauvignon Blanc

SERVE WITH   60-Minute Bread (page 207) or good store-bought bread; Simple Green Salad (page 196)

FRESH FENNEL is an especially good addition because you can add it in large enough quantity so that it becomes an essential component of the dish, not only for flavor but as a vegetable to round things out.

EVERY YEAR, we see more and more cultivated mussels, most often from Prince Edward Island, which is fast becoming the mussel-farming capital of North America. These are easy to clean (almost clean enough to eat without washing, but still worth a quick going-over), with very few rejects and plump meat. Wild mussels are tastier, but harder to clean. See page 61 for cleaning instructions.

Anise-Steamed Mussels, Asian Style: Combine the mussels in a cold pot with 1 cinnamon stick, 4 star anise, 2 tablespoons soy sauce, and 2 tablespoons water. Cover and cook until mussels open, 5 to 10 minutes. Toss, if possible, with about ½ cup torn Thai basil leaves (or use regular basil, chives, mint, or cilantro).

Plain Steamed Mussels: The procedure is the same, but omit all ingredients except mussels, oil, and garlic. These are great with a little melted butter (laced with minced garlic, if you like), drizzled over them when they're done.

| There are many, many herbs, spices, vegetables, and other seasonings that can lend a licorice flavor, including aniseeds or ground anise, five-spice powder, ouzo or raki (the anise-scented liqueurs of the eastern Mediterranean), and tarragon, chervil, even basil—especially Thai basil. (You could probably throw in a few pieces of Good 'n Plenty while you're at it.)

Crabby Crabcakes

TIME: 1 hour

MAKES: 4 servings

Somehow crabcakes have become an emblematic dish, as in "this restaurant has the best crabcakes." But since crab has the best texture and subtlest flavor of all of the crustaceans, the best crabcakes are those that showcase the crab most fully. And this means that getting the most out of crabcakes often means putting the least into them. When you start loading crabcakes up with white bread, corn, curry, and complicated sauces, you might be making them different, but you're not making them better.

1 pound fresh lump crabmeat
1 egg
1 tablespoon Dijon mustard, optional
Salt and freshly ground black pepper

2 tablespoons flour, plus flour for dredging
4 tablespoons extra virgin olive oil or neutral oil, such as canola or grapeseed
Lemon wedges

1 Gently combine the crabmeat, egg, mustard, if using, salt, pepper, and 2 tablespoons flour. Cover and put in the freezer for 5 minutes. Shape the mixture into four hamburger-shaped patties. Line a plate with plastic wrap and put the crabcakes on it. Cover with more plastic wrap and refrigerate for about 30 minutes (longer—up to a day—if you like) or freeze for 15 minutes.

2 Put the flour for dredging in a bowl. Pour the oil into a 12-inch skillet and turn the heat to medium. When the oil is hot, gently dredge one of the crabcakes in the flour. Gently tap off the excess flour and add the crabcake to the pan; repeat with the remaining crabcakes, then turn the heat to medium-high.

3 Cook, rotating the cakes in the pan as necessary to brown the first side, 5 to 8 minutes. Turn and brown the other side, which will take slightly less time. Serve hot, with lemon wedges.

WINE A lesser Cabernet or Bordeaux, Pinot Noir, or lighter wine from southern France

SERVE WITH Simple Green Salad (page 196) or salad with whatever sauce you are serving with the crabcakes (thinned a bit, if necessary, to use as salad dressing), or Tomato Salad with Basil (page 198)

START WITH picked lump or claw crabmeat, the biggest pieces from the body or claw. Mix gently so that some pieces retain their form, giving the crabcake a variety of textures.

PICKED CRABMEAT freezes fairly well; if you're unable to cook it immediately, throw it in the freezer for a few days. The quality of the thawed meat, at least when the crab is used in crabcakes, is nearly perfect.

IT'S BEST to chill the mix before shaping but, more important, it's essential to chill it for a half-hour or so (longer is even better) before cooking it. When cold, the cakes will hold together through cooking and, once the egg does its work, they will retain their shape—barely—until attacked with a fork.

Crabby Crabcakes with Tartar Sauce: Combine 1 cup mayonnaise (preferably home-made) with ¼ cup minced cornichons or other pickles, 2 tablespoons minced shallots, and horseradish to taste. Serve with the crabcakes.

Crabby Crabcakes with Aioli: Combine 1 cup mayonnaise (preferably homemade) with 1 tea-spoon finely minced raw garlic and a pinch saffron. Let rest for an hour or so before serving with crabcakes.

Crunchier Crabcakes: Add ½ cup or so of minced bell pepper (a combination of colors is nice) and/or some minced shallots or onions to the crabcake mix.

In place of the olive oil, use ¼ cup (½ stick) butter mixed with 2 tablespoons neutral oil. Heat until the butter foam subsides and then cook as above.

Southeast Asian Shrimp and Grapefruit Salad

TIME: 30 minutes
MAKES: 4 servings

Although lime is by far the most commonly used citrus fruit in Thai and other Southeast Asian cooking, grapefruit and its close relative, the pomelo, are often found in savory dishes, especially cool salads. And why not? Grapefruit adds distinctive flavor, unusual texture, and an impressive amount of juice. This is a nearly traditional salad in which the grapefruit plays a leading role, complementing the mild shrimp and allowing you to make an almost ridiculously easy dressing, comprising nothing more than nam pla (Thai fish sauce) or soy, lime, a bit of sugar, and some water.

1 to 1½ pounds unshelled shrimp

Salt

3 tablespoons nam pla (Thai fish sauce) or soy sauce

1 tablespoon sugar

Juice of 2 limes

6 cups torn lettuce or mesclun, washed and dried

2 grapefruit, peeled and sectioned, tough white pith removed, each section cut in half

¼ cup chopped fresh mint

¼ cup chopped fresh cilantro

Minced chiles or crushed red pepper flakes, optional

½ cup chopped dry-roasted peanuts, optional

1 Put the shrimp in a saucepan with salted water to cover. Bring to a boil, then turn off the heat and let sit for 5 minutes, or until the shrimp are opaque in the center. Cool in the refrigerator or under cold running water, then peel (and devein if you like). Cut the shrimp in half if they're large.

2 To make the dressing, combine the nam pla or soy with 2 tablespoons water, the sugar, and lime juice and blend or whisk until smooth.

3 Arrange the lettuce on four plates and top each portion with a few grapefruit pieces, some shrimp, and the mint and cilantro. Drizzle with the dressing, then sprinkle with a little chile and chopped peanuts, if you like, or pass them at the table.

WINE Beer or not-too-dry Riesling or Gewürztraminer
SERVE WITH Cold Noodles with Sesame (or Peanut) Sauce (page 210) or Stir-Fried Coconut Noodles (page 44)

USE GOOD SHRIMP—Pacific or Gulf whites are the best, though the less expensive and widely available tiger shrimp are acceptable—and buy them big, because you'll have fewer to peel. If you trust your fishmonger, you can even buy precooked, prepeeled shrimp, and save yourself a lot of trouble.

THE BEST WAY to retain the juices of the grapefruit is to peel and section it as you would an orange, not by cutting it in half and scooping out the flesh as you would to serve it at the table. Remove as much of the tough white pith as you can before cutting each section in two, which you should do just before assembling the salad.

Grilled Shrimp and Grapefruit Salad: Grill the shrimp, plain or basted with a flavorful sauce, like a combination of lime, ginger, garlic, soy, and peanut oil.

| Substitute Thai basil for either the mint or cilantro, or add it to the mix.

Cold Poached Shrimp with Marjoram "Pesto"

TIME: 30 minutes
MAKES: 4 servings

To make Italian-style herb pastes—like pesto—you take a great deal of a single herb (if you combine them you muddy the flavor) and pulverize it with olive oil and seasonings. The olive oil should be good, the seasonings should include salt, pepper, and garlic, and the rest of the guidelines are quite flexible. The idea, as with the familiar basil-based pesto, is to preserve, intensify, and complement the flavor of the herb, not transform or overwhelm it. Here's a paste based on marjoram, an unheralded herb that grows well in much of the country and can be found almost any place fresh herbs are sold. It perfectly complements cold poached shrimp.

1½ pounds shrimp, preferably not peeled

Salt

2 cups fresh marjoram, leaves and small stems only

1 large or 2 small garlic cloves, peeled

2 teaspoons red wine vinegar

⅓ cup extra virgin olive oil

1 tablespoon capers

2 anchovy fillets, optional

Freshly ground black pepper

1 Combine the shrimp in a saucepan with water to cover and a large pinch of salt. Bring to a boil and turn off the heat; let the shrimp cool in the water for about 5 minutes, or until the shrimp are opaque in the center. Rinse under cold running water until cool. Peel (and devein if you like), then arrange on a platter.

2 Combine the marjoram and garlic in a blender or small food processor. Process until finely minced, scraping down the sides with a rubber spatula once or twice if necessary. Add the vinegar and most of the oil and process until smooth.

3 Add the capers and anchovies, if using, and pulse the machine on and off a few times; you want to mince, not puree, the mixture, so don't overprocess.

4 Stir in the remaining oil, along with salt and pepper to taste. Serve the sauce with the cold shrimp.

WINE A white Burgundy or a nicely oaked California Chardonnay

SERVE WITH This salad can be built into a whole meal by garnishing it with an assortment of raw and partly cooked and chilled vegetables and other foods, like carrots, celery, artichokes, red bell peppers, hard-boiled eggs, and so on.

THIS SAUCE contains raw garlic, anchovies, and capers, a combination that reduces the need for ordinary salt to an absolute minimum; in fact, you shouldn't add any salt at all until you taste it.

YOU CAN BUY peeled shrimp, but shrimp poached in their shells have more flavor (as do shrimp poached in salt water; the water should taste salty). If you're going to peel the shrimp yourself, as I recommend, it pays to buy large shrimp and cut down on the work. Go for those in the range of 30 to 40 per pound (sometimes labeled "U-40" as in "under-40"), or even larger if the cost is not prohibitive.

MARJORAM IS related to and resembles oregano, but its flavor is better. Oregano is a good but not perfect substitute.

Cold Poached Scallops, Squid, or Octopus with Marjoram Pesto: Scallops, squid, and octopus are all good cold. Scallops may be cooked just like shrimp, but for a minute or two less, and squid should be cooked just until it loses its rubberiness, a minute or two; but octopus must be simmered for at least an hour to become tender.

| To subtly improve the flavor of the shrimp, add other seasonings to the poaching liquid—the easiest thing is to grab a handful of pickling mix, which usually contains peppercorns, allspice, bay leaf, coriander, and dill seeds. Throw in a couple of garlic cloves or a piece of onion if you like.

| You can substitute any herb for the marjoram, but the best (and most traditional) are basil, parsley, oregano, and mint.

| Some of the oil can be replaced by water. (Hot water will help preserve the color of the herb.)

| Other optional flavorings include pine nuts (pignolis), dry hard cheese, like Parmigiano-Reggiano or Pecorino Romano, chopped eggs, and pitted olives. These should not be pureed if possible but minced (or, in the case of cheese, grated) and added when the paste is already smooth.

Spanish-Style Shrimp

TIME: About 20 minutes
MAKES: 4 servings

Much of the flavor of shrimp can be lost in the cooking, especially when you're grilling or broiling, which allow the juices exuded by the shrimp to escape. Far better for preserving the crustacean's essence is cooking it in liquid, and among the best of those liquids is olive oil. This is not sautéing, but cooking the shrimp slowly in the oil, to tease out its liquids without evaporating them, so these juices combine with the oil to create an irresistible sauce.

⅓ cup extra virgin olive oil

3 or 4 big garlic cloves, cut into thin slivers

1 teaspoon ground cumin, or to taste

1 teaspoon paprika, or to taste

2 pounds unshelled shrimp, in the 15- to 20-per-pound range

Salt and freshly ground black pepper

¼ cup chopped fresh parsley leaves

1 Combine the oil and garlic in a 10- or 12-inch skillet. Turn the heat to medium and cook until the garlic begins to sizzle. Add the cumin and paprika. Stir, raise the heat to medium-high, and add the shrimp, along with some salt and pepper.

2 Cook, stirring occasionally, until the shrimp are all pink, no longer; you do not want to evaporate their liquid. Turn off the heat, add the parsley, and serve.

WINE Rioja or another red from northern Spain; for the scampi variation, try a crisp white like Orvieto or Pinot Grigio; the Asian variation is best with beer

SERVE WITH 60-Minute Bread (page 207) or good store-bought bread is essential; Simple Green Salad (page 196) is also nice.

I USUALLY PEEL shrimp before cooking, but in this instance the shrimp are better left unpeeled, for the simple reason that the peels contain as much flavor as the meat (maybe more), and you want that flavor in the sauce. The results are a little messier, and certainly more difficult to eat, but they are tastier—and the dish is easier to prepare.

THE KIND AND SIZE of shrimp is always a question for cooks, and here I recommend fairly large specimens, about 15 to 20 per pound. Pacific white shrimp, which come from southern California, Mexico, and the western shoulder of South America, are a good choice, as are Gulf white shrimp from the Gulf of Mexico. The less expensive farm-raised shrimp from Asia, like black tigers, are less flavorful, but they will still show very nicely in this dish.

Shrimp, Scampi-Style: Omit the cumin and paprika; use cayenne in place of black pepper. When the shrimp are cooked, stir in 2 or more tablespoons fresh lemon juice. Garnish with parsley and serve with lemon wedges.

Shrimp with Asian Flavors: Substitute peanut or vegetable oil for the olive oil and cook 1 tablespoon chopped ginger and 2 or 3 dried red chiles (or to taste) along with the garlic; omit the cumin and paprika. When the shrimp are done, stir in 1 tablespoon of soy sauce. Garnish with minced scallions or cilantro and serve with lime wedges.

Shrimp Cooked in Lime Juice

TIME: 20 to 30 minutes
MAKES: 4 servings

This is a Southeast Asian-style preparation, mildly sweet and mouth-puckeringly sour. It's also ridiculously fast; if you start some rice before tackling the shrimp, they will both be done at about the same time, 20 minutes later. (This assumes your shrimp are already peeled, a task that will take you about 10 minutes, and one that should be undertaken before cooking the rice.)

About ½ cup fresh lime juice (3 or 4 limes)

¼ cup sugar

1 tablespoon nam pla (Thai fish sauce), or salt to taste

2 tablespoons neutral oil, such as canola or grapeseed

1 teaspoon minced garlic

½ teaspoon crushed red pepper flakes, or to taste

1½ pounds peeled shrimp (deveined if you like), or 3 pounds head-on shrimp, left unpeeled

Minced cilantro

1 Combine the lime juice, sugar, and nam pla in a small bowl. Pour the oil into a 10- or 12-inch skillet, turn the heat to high, and heat for a minute. Add the garlic and pepper flakes and cook just until the garlic begins to brown about 5 minutes. Immediately add the lime juice mixture all at once and cook until it reduces by half, or even more, 3 to 5 minutes; there should be only about ¼ cup liquid in the skillet, and it should be syrupy.

2 Add the shrimp and cook, still over high heat. The shrimp will give off liquid of their own and begin to turn pink almost immediately. After about 2 minutes of cooking, stir. Continue cooking and stirring occasionally until all the shrimp are pink, about 2 more minutes. Taste and adjust the seasoning, then garnish with cilantro.

WINE Beer

SERVE WITH Easy Rice (page 204), and plenty of it, plus stir-fried vegetables or Green Salad with Soy Vinaigrette (page 197)

FOR BEST FLAVOR, see if you can find head-on shrimp; they make for a more impressive presentation; and it's fun to suck the juices out of the heads themselves (which, I realize, is not something that everyone enjoys). But none of these assets is worth making heads-on shrimp a sticking point.

BE SURE TO BROWN the garlic lightly without burning it.

LET THE LIME-SUGAR mixture cook until it is syrupy; this won't take long, just 3 minutes or so, but it will guarantee that the liquid coats the shrimp nicely.

NAM PLA—Thai fish sauce—is available in many supermarkets and all Asian food stores; soy sauce or even salt are adequate substitutes.

Scallops or Squid Cooked in Lime Juice: The same technique will work with scallops or cut-up squid; each will take slightly less time to cook than the shrimp.

Shrimp, Roman Style

This shrimp dish is based on a combination of ingredients that is traditionally used for cooking tripe in and around Rome. It's a simple tomato sauce spiked with the powerful flavors of garlic, chiles, and mint. When you make it with tripe, it must cook a long time in order for the tripe to become tender; when you use the shrimp, the dish is practically done as soon as they are added.

2 tablespoons extra virgin olive oil

1 tablespoon slivered or not-too-finely chopped garlic

6 dried red chiles or ½ teaspoon crushed red pepper flakes, or to taste

One 28-ounce can plum tomatoes, chopped, with their juice, or 4 cups chopped fresh tomatoes

Salt and freshly ground black pepper

2 pounds shrimp, peeled (and deveined, if you like)

1 cup chopped fresh mint leaves, or 1 tablespoon or more dried mint

1 Pour the olive oil into a large, deep skillet and turn the heat to medium. Add the garlic and chiles. When the garlic begins to color, about 3 minutes later, cook carefully until it browns just a bit. Turn the heat off for a minute to avoid spattering, then add the tomatoes.

2 Turn the heat to medium-high and bring to a boil, then reduce the heat to medium and simmer, stirring occasionally. Add salt and pepper to taste.

3 Add the shrimp and cook, stirring occasionally, until they are all pink, 5 to 10 minutes. Taste and adjust the seasoning; the sauce should be quite strong. Stir in the mint and serve.

WINE Chianti or any not-too-serious wine from Italy or France

SERVE WITH If you're not making pasta (see above), serve with 60-Minute Bread (page 207) or good store-bought bread and Simple Green Salad (page 196).

THE GARLIC in the sauce is not cut too finely, and it is browned nearly to the point of bitterness to make it extra strong.

THE SAUCE itself is cooked just long enough for the tomatoes to juice up and begin to fall apart; it should not be allowed to become too dry because the final product should be a moist, almost soupy stew, rather than shrimp coated in a thick paste.

MINT IS the star component here. (Mint grows wild in the hills around Rome and is featured in a number of classic dishes.) Dried mint will do—add it a couple of minutes before the sauce is done—but given that fresh mint is readily available I strongly recommend using it.

Shrimp, Roman Style, with Pasta: The consistency of the sauce makes the dish ideal as a topping for pasta. Just cut the amount of shrimp to about a pound—with a pound of pasta as the base, there's no need for more than that. Start the water for the pasta when you start the sauce, and begin to cook the pasta at the same time as the shrimp.

Squid or Scallops, Roman Style: The same procedure can be followed to make this dish using cut-up squid (which should be cooked just until tender, probably even less time than the shrimp) or scallops, which will take about the same time as shrimp.

Shrimp with Better Cocktail Sauce

No doubt shrimp with cocktail sauce is a luxury dish, but it has sunk to the point where too frequently it means a pile of shrimp cooked days in advance, served on a bed of iceberg lettuce with some bottled sauce that always needs more help than it ever receives. There is a better way, however. Cook the shrimp yourself; in the meantime, prepare a simple ketchup-based sauce that has so much flavor, you'll find it becoming a part of your standard repertoire.

About 2 pounds large shrimp, peeled (and deveined, if you like)

1 cup ketchup

1 tablespoon red wine or other vinegar

3 tablespoons butter

2 tablespoons prepared horseradish, or to taste

1 Combine the shrimp in a saucepan with water to cover. Turn the heat to high and bring to a boil. Cover the pan, remove from the heat, and let sit for 5 minutes. Drain and chill (you can run the shrimp under cold water if you're in a hurry).

2 Combine the ketchup, vinegar, and butter in a small saucepan and cook over medium-low heat, stirring occasionally, until the butter melts. (At this point, you can keep the sauce warm for an over—but keep the heat as low as possible.) Add horseradish to taste.

3 Serve the cold shrimp with the sauce, warm or cold.

WINE Chardonnay or Pinot Blanc

SERVE WITH If you serve this as an appetizer, follow with pasta like Pasta alla Gricia (page 28) or risotto. If you serve this as a main course, serve with bread, like 60-Minute Bread (page 207) and a steamed vegetable, like Steamed Broccoli (or Other Vegetable) (page 203).

Keys To SUCCESS

THE EASIEST WAY to cook shrimp is to let them steep in hot water until they're done; they will cook through but not overcook, and thus remain tender. Peel them before cooking.

SEE SPANISH-STYLE SHRIMP (page 71) for recommendations about buying shrimp.

With MINIMAL Effort

| If you have fresh horseradish, grate it and serve it separately from the sauce; dip the shrimp into the ketchup sauce and then into the horseradish.

| Use fresh lemon juice instead of vinegar, and/or Tabasco or other hot sauce in place of the horseradish.

| Cook the shrimp with herbs or spices, such as a premixed combination of pickling spices, or simply a couple of bay leaves, some peppercorns, and some whole coriander seeds.

Shrimp in "Barbecue" Sauce

TIME: 15 to 30 minutes
MAKES: 4 servings

This is an old New Orleans recipe that has nothing to do with grilling or barbecuing. Its name comes from the spicy, slightly smoky flavor the shrimp gain when cooked with Worcestershire sauce and lots of black pepper. It's a fine and almost absurdly fast dish—once the shrimp are peeled, you can have it on the table in 10 minutes, and that's not an exaggeration—with a creamy, rich, savory sauce that completely belies the amount of effort required on your part.

¼ cup (½ stick) butter

1½ to 2 pounds shrimp, peeled (and deveined, if you like)

2 tablespoons Worcestershire or soy sauce

Salt

½ teaspoon freshly ground black pepper, or more to taste

Juice of 1 lemon

1 Put the butter in a skillet and turn the heat to high. When the butter melts, add the shrimp and Worcestershire sauce. Cook, stirring occasionally, until the sauce is glossy and thick and the shrimp uniformly pink, about 5 minutes. If at any point the sauce threatens to dry out, add 1 to 2 tablespoons water.

2 When the shrimp are done, season with salt and pepper, then stir in the lemon juice and serve.

WINE Any simple, inexpensive red
SERVE WITH 60-Minute Bread (page 207) or good store-bought bread, Easy Rice (page 204), or Pasta, Risotto-Style (page 26); Steamed Broccoli (or Other Vegetable) (page 203)

Keys To SUCCESS

THE KEY INGREDIENT here is butter. If you start with a moderate amount of butter, about a tablespoon per serving of shrimp, you can add almost any flavor you like to the skillet and create a sauce with the same creaminess and great depth of flavor. (This is not a place where substituting oil is a good idea; you'll never get anything approaching the same texture.)

IN A NARROW PAN, the liquid seasoning and shrimp juices will evaporate more slowly; you'll need less liquid to prevent the sauce from being too watery. In a wide one, however, the liquids evaporate quite rapidly, and there's even a danger of burning. In this case, add a tablespoon or two of water, which will keep the sauce at the right consistency.

GENERALLY, I ADVOCATE buying wild shrimp, like Pacific or Gulf whites, which are the best. In this instance, however, you can get away with the far less expensive farm-raised shrimp, like black tigers—the sauce has so much flavor that no matter what seasoning you use, the subtleties of better shrimp would be lost.

With MINIMAL Effort

| Use 3 tablespoons red wine vinegar in place of the Worcestershire sauce; omit the lemon juice.

| Use 2 tablespoons Dijon-style mustard and 1 tablespoon water in place of the Worcestershire sauce.

Spicy Shrimp

Next to scallops, shrimp are probably the easiest animals to cook, and the fastest. This dish is among my favorites, great grilled in the summer, but also perfect when broiled or roasted. Despite its name, it isn't fiery hot, but the addition of a fair amount of paprika gives the shrimp a bright red color that makes people think they're eating spicy food, but without getting the tops of their heads blown off.

1 large garlic clove
1 tablespoon coarse salt
½ teaspoon cayenne
1 teaspoon medium-to-mild paprika
2 tablespoons olive oil
2 teaspoons fresh lemon juice
1½ to 2 pounds shrimp, peeled (and deveined, if you like)
Lemon wedges

1 Start a hot charcoal or wood fire, preheat a gas grill to the maximum, preheat the broiler with the rack close to the heat source, or preheat the oven to 500°F.

2 Mince the garlic with the salt. Mix in the cayenne and paprika, then make into a paste with the oil and lemon juice. Smear the paste on the shrimp. Grill, broil, or roast the shrimp for 2 to 3 minutes a side, turning once. Serve immediately or at room temperature, with lemon wedges.

WINE A gutsy red, like Zinfandel or Côtes du Rhône
SERVE WITH Simple Green Salad (page 196), Tomato Salad with Basil (page 198), Raw Beet Salad (page 194), or any other fresh salad

THE REAL KEY HERE is fresh paprika, not that tin you inherited from your mother. After you buy it, taste it; if it is hot, use half a teaspoon.

YOU CAN LET the shrimp sit in the spice paste for hours. (In fact, I like to dump both shrimp and paste in a covered plastic container, shake them together to coat the shrimp, then carry the container to a party and grill the shrimp there.) But you can also just mix the two together right before cooking.

IF YOU DON'T WANT to grill, broil the shrimp, as close to the heat source as possible; turn them once. Or roast them at 500°F (or the maximum temperature for your oven), shaking the pan once or twice. In either case, cooking time will be 5 to 10 minutes.

| Substitute chili or curry powder for the paprika, peanut oil for the olive oil, and lime juice for the lemon juice.

Scallops "a la Plancha"

TIME: 20 minutes
MAKES: 4 servings

The scallop counts among its assets not only great flavor and texture but speed in cooking. Since scallops are shucked right after harvest, and the muscle separated from the viscera, they are the safest bivalves to eat raw, or rare. This makes the scallop ideal for fast cooking, because even a large scallop needs only to be browned on both sides. A good sear on the outside caramelizes the shellfish's natural sugars and leaves the interior cool, creamy, and delicious.

I like this traditional Catalonian method. *A la plancha*, refers to the large, flat griddle used to sear the fish. A cast-iron or nonstick skillet works equally well, as long as the pan is very, very hot.

1½ pounds sea or bay scallops

1 garlic clove, peeled and lightly crushed

2 tablespoons extra virgin olive oil

1 tablespoon sherry vinegar

Salt and freshly ground black pepper

Minced fresh parsley

1 Toss the scallops and the garlic on a plate and drizzle with the oil and vinegar; sprinkle with salt and pepper and turn over a couple of times. Go about your business for 5 minutes.

2 Put a large, preferably nonstick, skillet over high heat. When the skillet smokes—this will take a couple of minutes—add the scallops (leave the liquid behind), a few at a time. By the time you've added the last scallop, the first one will probably be browned on one side, so begin turning them. Cook until brown on both sides but still rare in the center. (You must work more quickly with bay scallops—add them a few at a time, and turn them quickly; you may even have to work in batches to keep them from becoming overcooked.)

3 Serve hot, drizzled with the juices from the plate and garnished with the parsley.

WINE Albariño (the great Spanish white); light, dry Gewürztraminer or Riesling; crisp Muscadet; or real Chablis

SERVE WITH 60-Minute Bread (page 207), good store-bought bread, or Olive Oil Croutons (page 208); Simple Green Salad (make the dressing with sherry vinegar) (page 196)

PREHEAT THE SKILLET for at least 2 minutes before beginning to cook—it should be so hot that the scallop's muscle contracts quickly enough to literally jump when it hits the surface.

TURN ON YOUR exhaust fan if you have one; this generates a fair amount of smoke. (Fortunately the cooking time is minimal.)

REAL BAY SCALLOPS, available only in winter, are best. Otherwise use sea scallops. Always ask for "dry" scallops: those that have not been soaked in preservatives.

Shrimp or Squid a la Plancha: This technique works perfectly with both shrimp and squid. Keep the cooking time especially short for squid or it will become tough.

| Vary the kind of oil, vinegar, seasoning, and garnish as you like. For example, use peanut oil with scallions and ginger, then garnish with a drizzle of soy sauce or cilantro for a completely different take.

Curried Scallops with Tomatoes

TIME: 20 to 30 minutes
MAKES: 4 servings

You can never go wrong by adding a little crunch to scallops when you sauté them. Usually, you dredge them in flour, cornmeal, or bread crumbs before adding them to the hot pan, and it's something that most everyone seems to like. But you can take that crunch and give it an intense flavor by dredging the scallops directly in a spice mix. Although you can't do this with everything—dried herbs don't get crisp, and some spices are far too strong to use in this quantity—it works perfectly with curry powder, which not only seasons the scallops and their accompanying sauce but gives them the crunch we all crave.

3 medium ripe tomatoes

1 tablespoon peanut or vegetable oil

1½ to 2 pounds large sea scallops

Salt and freshly ground black pepper

2 tablespoons curry powder, or to taste

½ cup heavy cream, sour cream, or yogurt, optional

Juice of 1 lime

½ cup washed, dried and chopped fresh cilantro

1 Core the tomatoes (cut a cone-shaped wedge out of the stem end), then cut them in half horizontally. Gently squeeze out the liquid and shake out most of their seeds. Chop their flesh into ½-inch pieces and set aside. Heat a 12-inch nonstick skillet over medium heat for about 3 minutes. While it is heating, sprinkle the scallops with salt and pepper and spread the curry powder on a plate.

2 Add the oil, then quickly dredge the scallops lightly in the curry powder and add them to the pan. About 2 minutes after you added the first scallop, turn it—it should be nicely browned (if it is not, raise the heat a bit). When the scallops are all browned and turned, cook for another minute, then add the tomatoes and the cream if you're using it (if you are using yogurt, lower the heat immediately; it must not boil).

3 Heat the tomatoes through, then taste and add more salt and pepper if necessary. Sprinkle with the lime juice, stir in the cilantro, and serve.

WINE Inexpensive, rugged red, like Zinfandel or Syrah from California, no-name wine from the south of France, or Chianti

SERVE WITH Easy Rice (page 204) or Stir-Fried Coconut Noodles (page 44); Simple Green Salad (page 196)

SINCE YOU'RE USING a large quantity of curry powder here, it should not be super-hot. (This is obviously a matter of taste, but I prefer a mild, sweet curry.) The powder itself must be fairly fine; if it is too coarse, the resulting crust will be gritty rather than crisp.

DREDGE THE SCALLOPS lightly in the curry, not as heavily as you would in flour.

KEEP THE SCALLOPS rare; they're at their best that way, and perfectly safe, as long as they're fresh.

Chile Scallops with Tomatoes: Use ground chili powder or any other spice mix in place of the curry.

Cilantro is the natural choice here—it marries perfectly with the lime and curry powder—but basil, especially the fragrant, minty Thai basil, is a more surprising and equally delicious option.

Scallops with Almonds

Scallops are tender, fast cooking, low-fat, and flavorful—a natural choice for weeknight cooking. There are dozens of simple scallop preparations, beginning with searing the scallops and serving them with lemon, and continuing with those recipes that rely on pan sauces, quick additions to the skillet after the scallops are cooked. These take advantage of the plentiful caramelized sugars left behind by the seared scallops, integrating them into the sauce and making sure that none of the mollusks' original flavors are lost. Here, a small handful of almonds adds contrasting texture as well as rich, deep color. The procedure is easy—for a 15-minute dish you cannot do much better.

1 tablespoon extra virgin olive oil

2 tablespoons butter

About 1½ pounds sea scallops

Salt

Pinch cayenne

⅓ cup roughly chopped almonds, skin on

¾ cup dry white wine

Chopped parsley leaves, optional

1 Combine the oil and 1 tablespoon of the butter in a large, preferably nonstick, skillet and turn the heat to medium-high. Sprinkle the scallops with salt and a bit of cayenne. When the butter foam subsides, add the scallops to the skillet, one at a time (or all at once if you're using bay scallops), and turn the heat to high. Cook for about 2 minutes, or until brown on one side, then turn and brown the other side for another 1 to 2 minutes. (Scallops are best when rare in the center; if you like them better done, cook for another couple of minutes.)

2 Remove the scallops to a plate and keep warm. Add the nuts to the skillet and, still over high heat, cook, stirring, until dark brown, just a minute or two. Add the wine and cook, stirring occasionally, until reduced to a syrup, about 5 minutes. Add the remaining 1 tablespoon butter. When it has thickened the sauce, pour over the scallops, garnish with parsley, and serve.

WINE Decent Bordeaux, Châteauneuf-du-Pape, or Meritage or Cabernet from California

SERVE WITH Bread, rice, another cooked grain, polenta, or Mashed Potatoes (page 205), along with Simple Green Salad (page 196) or Steamed Broccoli (or Other Vegetable) (page 203)

IF YOU CAN find the rare (and shockingly expensive) true bay scallops from Nantucket or Long Island, by all means use them, but reduce the cooking time for the smaller bays. Do not, however, try this dish with the tiny calico scallops which, despite your best efforts, will overcook before they brown.

| Walnuts and pecans work just as well as almonds; both add beautiful color and wonderful texture.

| Use red wine in place of white; the color will be even deeper, the flavor richer, and the wine pairing easier.

Triple Sesame Salad with Scallops

TIME: 40 minutes
MAKES: 4 servings

The perfect whole-meal salad features as much flavor, texture, and bulk as any other well-prepared meal, and the fact that the base is a pile of greens makes me feel like I'm getting away with something. This one takes about 10 minutes longer to prepare than a plain green salad, and, by changing the topping, can be made in different ways every time, always with a minimum of effort. My first choice for topping this salad is grilled scallops—they're almost ludicrously fast and easy, and their texture and flavor complement both greens and dressing.

¼ cup soy sauce

¼ cup rice wine or other vinegar

2 tablespoons sesame tahini or smooth peanut butter

1 tablespoon toasted sesame oil

¼ teaspoon crushed red pepper flakes, cayenne, or ground chile powder, or to taste

1 tablespoon honey

½ teaspoon chopped garlic

1 teaspoon peeled and chopped ginger

1½ to 2 pounds sea scallops

Salt

6 to 8 cups mesclun or any salad greens, washed and dried

¼ cup torn Thai or other basil, optional

2 tablespoons toasted sesame seeds

1 Prepare a gas or charcoal grill. Combine the soy sauce, vinegar, tahini, sesame oil, red pepper, honey, garlic, and ginger in a blender and purée until smooth. When the grill is hot, sprinkle the scallops with salt and grill them for about 2 minutes per side; they should remain tender and undercooked in the middle.

2 Combine the greens and basil and divide among four plates. When the scallops are done, top the greens with them, then drizzle with the dressing; sprinkle with the sesame seeds, and serve.

WINE Just-off-dry Gewürztraminer or Riesling, either from Germany or the Pacific Northwest, or good beer

SERVE WITH Crisp Pan-Fried Noodle Cake (page 212) or savory rice-based pancakes

THE TIMING OF this recipe is one of its real beauties. Start the grill (or heat a pan on top of the stove), and, while it's heating, make the dressing and wash the greens. When all else is ready, grill the scallops. It all works seamlessly, and incredibly quickly.

USE A BLENDER for the dressing; it makes quick work of dispersing the sesame paste or peanut butter throughout the liquid ingredients—something that can be a real hassle with a fork or a whisk—creating a perfect emulsion. Because the blender purées the garlic and ginger, there's no need to mince them; just peel, chop roughly, and drop them into the blender with the other ingredients.

YOU NEED NOT GRILL the scallops. They can be cooked on top of the stove in a grill pan or regular skillet; if you use a nonstick skillet you can cook with no oil at all.

TOAST SESAME SEEDS in a dry skillet over medium heat, shaking the pan occasionally, until they darken, about 5 minutes.

Triple Sesame Salad with Shrimp, Steak, or Chicken: Shrimp and steak are also great on these greens, as is boneless chicken—preferably thighs, which have better flavor than breasts and are less likely to dry out over the heat of the grill.

| Use any greens mix you like, although a premade, prewashed mesclun is obviously the easiest.

Squid in Red Wine Sauce

TIME: 1 to 1¼ hours, largely unattended

MAKES: 4 servings

This is my favorite dish using this plentiful but still-underappreciated cephalopod. (The term, which is also used for octopus and cuttlefish, describes sea creatures whose "feet" grow from their heads.) Like many people, I'm a fan of fried "calamari," but that dish is best suited to restaurants because of squid's tendency to spatter when deep-fried. Although sautéing or stir-frying are good, fast techniques for squid, they, too, tend to be messy. A gentle braise in flavorful liquid and seasonings is the perfect alternative, and this one, with its Provençal spirit, is delicious and warming.

3 tablespoons extra virgin olive oil

5 garlic cloves, crushed

2 pounds cleaned squid, the bodies cut up if large

1 cup fruity red wine, like Côtes du Rhône

Several sprigs fresh thyme, or 1 teaspoon dried

Salt and freshly ground black pepper

Chopped fresh parsley, optional

1 Put 2 tablespoons of the olive oil in a large skillet and turn the heat to medium-high. Add the garlic and cook, stirring, until lightly browned, 3 to 5 minutes. Add the squid and stir, then lower the heat and add the wine. Stir, add the thyme, and cover.

2 Cook at a slow simmer until the squid is tender, about 45 minutes. Uncover, season to taste, raise the heat, and cook until most but not all of the liquid is evaporated, 5 to 10 minutes. Stir in the remaining 1 tablespoon oil, garnish with the parsley if using, and serve.

WINE Whatever you use for cooking

SERVE WITH 60-Minute Bread (page 207) or good store-bought bread, or polenta; Sautéed Shiitake Mushrooms (page 202), and/or Simple Green Salad (page 196)

ALMOST ALL SQUID is sold so clean it just needs a quick rinse to be ready for cutting up and cooking; some of it is even sold cut into rings. To make it even more convenient, squid, like shrimp, is one of those rare seafoods whose quality barely suffers when frozen, so you can safely tuck a 2-pound bag into the freezer and let it sit for a month or two, defrosting it the day you're ready to cook. (Like shrimp, it will defrost quickly and safely when covered with cold water.)

Squid in Red Wine Sauce with Potatoes: Add some crisp sautéed potatoes or croutons of bread to the finished dish for a contrasting texture.

Squid in Red Wine Sauce with Tomatoes: Add a few chopped tomatoes (canned are fine) to make the sauce a bit thicker and more plentiful (in which case, you might as well serve the dish over pasta).

| Add fennel seeds or crushed red chiles to alter the flavor entirely.

Fish

Simplest Steamed Fish

If you have forgotten how delicious a fillet of fish can be, do this: Steam it, with nothing. Drizzle it with olive oil and lemon. Sprinkle it with salt. Eat it. If the number of ingredients and technique are minimal, the challenge is not. You need a near-perfect piece of fish to begin with, your timing must be precise—which is all a matter of attention and judgment, really—and your olive oil flavorful. That taken care of, there is no better or easier preparation.

1½ pounds cod or other fillet, in 2 pieces, or 1 large halibut steak

2 tablespoons extra virgin olive oil

Juice of ½ lemon

Coarse salt

1 Pour at least 1 inch of water into the bottom of a steamer (see Keys to Success), cover, and bring to a boil. Put the fish on the steamer's rack, making sure the rack is elevated above the water. Cover and steam for 4 to 8 minutes, or until the fish is done. (A good-sized halibut fillet may require 10 or even 12 minutes.)

2 Remove the fish to a warm platter and drizzle with olive oil and lemon juice. Sprinkle with coarse salt and serve.

WINE Muscadet, Pinot Grigio, or another light, fresh, white

SERVE WITH Start with pasta like Linguine with Tomato-Anchovy Sauce (page 40) or a soup. Serve with Simple Green Salad (page 196) or Glazed Carrots (page 201).

IN ADDITION TO perfect freshness, there is one other qualification for the fish: It must not be too thin. Steaming is such a fast technique that thin fillets inevitably overcook. So flounder is out, as are small fillets from most fish. The best thickness for steaming is about an inch.

FEW FILLETS are of uniform thickness; cod, for example, has both thick and thin ends. You can either remove the thin end (or ends, if there are more than one fillet) and save them for another use, or fold the thin end under itself to approximate the density of the thick end (this works). Obviously, you will not have this kind of problem with a halibut steak.

TO JURY-RIG a steaming vessel, I use a large, oval casserole with a rack that fits in it; it was designed for roasting meat. Since the rack only sits about ¼ inch above the bottom, though, I have to elevate it, which I do by resting it on a couple of glass ramekins. As long as you have a large rack that fits inside a larger pot you will figure something out.

FINALLY, THERE IS timing. Steaming is quick; sometimes 4 minutes is enough. You must check often—taking care not to scald yourself when removing the steamer's lid—and stop the cooking the instant a thin-bladed knife meets no resistance when poking the fillet.

Simplest Steamed Fish with Soy: You can drizzle the fish with anything you like in place of the olive oil and lemon. Try, for example, a drizzle of soy sauce and a little minced ginger and/or chopped scallion.

| This technique works beautifully not only with cod and halibut, but with red snapper, grouper, striped bass, sea bass, and even mackerel.

Fish Braised with Leeks

TIME: 30 minutes
MAKES: 4 servings

This is a dish that is almost too simple to believe, one that combines wonderful textures and flavors with a minimum of ingredients, no added fat, and almost no preparation or cooking time. Like the best minimalist dishes, everything counts here: the fish, the leeks—which remain crisp and assertive thanks to the quick cooking time—and even the wine or stock. For those who would prefer a little more potency in the dish, Dijon mustard provides a bit of a kick.

1½ pounds leeks, trimmed, chopped, and washed

½ cup dry white wine or chicken or fish stock

Salt and freshly ground black pepper

1 tablespoon Dijon mustard, optional

About 1½ pounds cod, salmon, or other fish fillet, about 1 inch thick

1 Preheat the oven to 400°F. Scatter the leeks over the bottom of an ovenproof casserole. Mix with the wine, salt, pepper, and optional mustard. Top with the fish; sprinkle the fish with salt and pepper. Cover the casserole.

2 Bake for 10 to 15 minutes, or until a thin-bladed knife meets little or no resistance when inserted into the thickest part of the fish. Uncover and serve the fish with the leeks and pan juices spooned over it.

WINE Crisp Chardonnay—real Chablis would be ideal—or a glass of hard sparkling cider

SERVE WITH 60-Minute Bread (page 207), good store-bought bread, Olive Oil Croutons (page 208), or Easy Rice (page 204)

YOU NEED A tightly covered container to preserve all the liquid and flavors inherent in this dish, but that can be as simple as a pot with a good-fitting lid or a lidded glass casserole—anything that prevents moisture from escaping.

LEEKS ARE the preferred member of the onion family because they remain crisp and their flavor is strong but not overwhelming; thinly sliced onions rings will do the job nearly as well. If you choose to use leeks, trim about ½ inch from the root end, then trim off all tough green leaves. Cut them in half lengthwise and chop; then wash well in a colander, making sure to rinse between all the layers.

Chicken Braised with Leeks: Follow the recipe exactly, substituting boneless chicken breasts for the fish. Cooking time will be just about the same.

Shrimp Baked with Leeks: Because shrimp cooks so quickly, it's worth baking the leeks for 5 minutes first. Then put the shrimp on top and bake for an additional 10 minutes or so.

| Substitute a couple of cups of chopped tomato for the leeks; or add some in addition to the leeks. In this instance you can reduce or nearly eliminate the added stock or wine—or just use a sprinkling of olive oil or fresh lemon juice.

| In place of the mustard, try soy sauce, chopped fresh herbs (a couple of teaspoons of thyme leaves, for example), or a teaspoon of curry powder or another spice mix.

Roast Fish with Crisp Potatoes, Olives, and Bay Leaves

TIME: 40 to 50 minutes

MAKES: 4 servings

Aside from the fish, you probably have on hand everything you need to make this dish, which begins with cooking thin-sliced potatoes in good olive oil. Add a handful of bay leaves, fillets of sturdy white fish, and a lot of black olives. The result is crisp potatoes and tender fish with luxuriously juicy olives.

2 large baking potatoes (about 1 pound)

½ cup extra virgin olive oil

Salt and freshly ground black pepper

15 bay leaves

1 cup black olives

1½ pounds monkfish or other fillets

1 Preheat the oven to 400°F. Peel and thinly slice the potatoes (use a mandoline if you have one). Oil the bottom of a 9 × 13-inch baking pan with ¼ cup oil; top with a single layer of the potatoes (it's okay if they overlap a little). Season with salt and pepper and top with the bay leaves and the remaining ¼ cup oil.

2 Roast for 10 minutes. Check and turn the pan back to front, shaking it a little to bathe the potatoes in oil. Roast for 10 minutes more. At this point the potatoes should be browning; if not, roast for 5 minutes more.

3 Top the potatoes with the olives and the fish; sprinkle the fish with salt and pepper. Roast for 10 minutes more, or until the fish is tender, but not overcooked. Serve immediately.

WINE A Beaujolais, a light Pinot Noir, or a crisp, high-acid white, like Graves, or a well-made Sauvignon Blanc

SERVE WITH Simple Green Salad (page 196) or Steamed Broccoli (or Other Vegetable) (page 203)

THE COMBINATION of high-heat roasting and plenty of olive oil is the easiest and most foolproof method for getting crisp potatoes. The quantity of potatoes must necessarily be limited or they will not brown properly.

ALTHOUGH ANY black olives will work, the best to use here are good-quality oil-cured olives, the small, shriveled kind. They soften and plump up a bit, and their bitterness is greatly tamed by cooking.

THE STURDY texture of monkfish is ideal for roasting, but certain other fillets will give similar results: red snapper, sea bass, pollock, wolffish, even catfish. And even more delicate fillets, from cod to bluefish, are suitable.

IT'S BEST to remove the thin membrane clinging to the monkfish before cooking. Just pull and tug on it while cutting through it with a paring knife and it will come off; you don't have to be too compulsive about this task, but try to get most of it off.

LARGE PIECES of monkfish—those weighing more than a pound—should be split down the middle lengthwise to make two fillets before cooking.

FINALLY, UNLIKE most white-fleshed fish, monkfish requires thorough cooking, to the point where it is opaque and tender throughout. You'll know it's done when a thin-bladed knife inserted into the thickest part meets little resistance.

| You can mix sliced onions or other root vegetables in with the potatoes, and the results will be delicious, but the juices of the vegetables will reduce the potatoes' browning; it's a trade-off, and there's nothing to be done about it.

| Substitute about 10 sprigs of thyme for the bay leaves; or use about 2 teaspoons fresh (or 1 teaspoon dried) rosemary.

| Other possibilities: 1 tablespoon ground cumin or cumin seeds, 1 tablespoon fennel seeds, 3 teaspoons curry powder (sprinkle 1 teaspoon on the fish itself), a few threads of saffron, or 1 tablespoon good, medium-hot paprika.

Roast Fish with Meat Sauce

Back in the old days, when I was a cooking fanatic, I made a wonderful roasted monkfish recipe. The sauce was a reduction that began with meat bones, continued with roasted vegetables, and required four or five steps over a two-day period.

Now, I make the same sauce with pan-roasted vegetables, a simple combination of onion, carrot, and celery, darkly browned in a little bit of butter, and a can of beef stock. It takes a half-hour or less, and although it doesn't have the richness of my original work of art, no one to whom I served both could tell the difference with certainty.

1 tablespoon butter

1 small carrot, roughly chopped

1 celery stalk, roughly chopped

1 small onion, roughly chopped

1 tablespoon tomato paste, optional

One 13-ounce can beef broth, or 1½ cups meat or chicken stock

1½ to 2 pounds monkfish

Salt and freshly ground black pepper

1 teaspoon extra virgin olive oil

1 Preheat the oven to 500°F (or its maximum temperature). Put a cast-iron or other ovenproof skillet or roasting pan in the oven while it is heating. Put 1½ teaspoons butter in a small saucepan and turn the heat to medium-high. When the butter is melted, add the carrot and celery and stir; a minute later, add the onion. Cook, stirring occasionally, until the vegetables brown—be careful not to let them burn—less than 10 minutes. Stir in the tomato paste if you're using it, then the broth. Bring to a boil, then adjust the heat so the mixture simmers for about 10 minutes.

2 Strain the broth, pressing on the vegetables to extract their liquid. Return the broth to medium-high heat and bring to a boil. Boil until reduced by about three-quarters, or until less than ½ cup of thick liquid remains.

3 Meanwhile, season the fish with salt and pepper. Carefully remove the hot pan from the oven and pour in the oil; swirl to coat the bottom of the pan. Add the fish and roast for 5 minutes. Remove from the oven and

WINE A first-class Bordeaux, Cabernet Sauvignon, or Barbaresco

SERVE WITH 60-Minute Bread (page 207) or good store-bought bread; Simple Green Salad (page 196); Mashed Potatoes (page 205), Crisp Potatoes (page 206), or roasted or Lyonnaise potatoes

carefully pour the liquid that has accumulated around the fish into the sauce. Once again, bring the sauce to a boil and reduce until it is thick, syrupy, and about ½ cup in volume. Turn the fish and roast it for another 5 minutes, or until a thin-bladed knife inserted into its thickest part meets little resistance.

4 Stir the remaining 1½ teaspoons butter into the sauce, then serve the fish with the sauce spooned over it.

when a thin-bladed knife inserted into the thickest part meets little resistance.

THE STURDY texture of monkfish is ideal for roasting, but certain other fillets will give similar results: red snapper, sea bass, pollock, wolffish, even catfish. And even more delicate fillets, from cod to bluefish, are suitable.

Keys To SUCCESS

A SPOONFUL of tomato paste added to the browned vegetables provides smoothness, body, and color; it's entirely optional.

IT'S BEST to remove the thin membrane clinging to the monkfish before cooking. Just pull and tug on it while cutting through it with a paring knife and it will come off; you don't have to be too compulsive about this task, but try to get most of it off.

LARGE PIECES of monkfish—those weighing more than a pound—should be split down the middle lengthwise to make two fillets before cooking.

FINALLY, UNLIKE most white-fleshed fish, monkfish requires thorough cooking, to the point where it is opaque and tender throughout. You'll know it's done

With MINIMAL Effort

Roast Monkfish with Asian Meat Sauce: To season the stock with Asian aromatic vegetables rather than traditional European ones, substitute 10 slices ginger, a stalk of lemongrass, and 5 scallions for the carrot, celery, and onion. Omit the tomato paste.

This will work with almost any meaty, white-fleshed fish, like halibut, catfish, striped bass, or sea bass. If you're careful not to overroast, it is also nice with more delicate fish, such as cod and haddock.

Fish Simmered in Spicy Soy Sauce

TIME: 20 minutes
MAKES: 4 servings

Good soy sauce makes a fine and instant poaching liquid, to which you can a variety of simple seasonings—here I use scallions and chile. Simmered in this, the fish gains not only the flavor of soy but a beautiful mahogany color. The dish can be garnished with the cooked scallions, and the poaching liquid—slightly reduced, but now enhanced by the flavor of the fish—makes a wonderful dressing for rice.

⅓ to ½ cup good soy sauce

2 teaspoons sugar

About 15 scallions, trimmed and cut into 2-inch lengths, or 1 large onion, sliced

1 dried or fresh chile, optional

One 1½-pound striped bass fillet, preferably a center cut

1 Combine the soy, ½ to 1 cup water, sugar, scallions, and optional chile in a deep skillet just large enough to hold the fish. Turn the heat to medium-high and bring to a boil.

2 Add the fish and adjust the heat so the mixture bubbles but not furiously. Cook for about 10 minutes, turning the fish once or twice, until it is coated with a brown glaze and cooked through. Serve the fish with white rice, spooning the sauce over all and garnishing with the scallions.

WINE Cold sake, beer, or Champagne

SERVE WITH Easy Rice (page 204) or Crisp Pan-fried Noodle Cake (page 212); Steamed Broccoli (or Other Vegetable) (page 203)

THERE IS a judgment to make here, and it can only be determined by tasting the soy sauce you're about to use. If it is mild, almost sweet—the kind you would happily use as a plain dip for sushi—you can dilute it with an equal amount of water. But if it is strong and highly salty, use 2 parts water to 1 part soy.

STRIPED BASS is meaty and flavorful, but you can use this preparation for cod, (undercook it slightly or it will fall apart), monkfish (cook a little longer to ensure tenderness), salmon, red snapper, sea bass, halibut, swordfish, or even sea scallops (which should be cooked for only 3 or 4 minutes). No matter which fish you choose, try to get a piece that is equally thick at both ends—this is easiest if you get a cut from the center of a large fillet—or the thin end will be overcooked before the thick end is done. The other alternative is to buy fish steaks, like salmon, swordfish, or halibut.

Fish and Shallots Simmered in Spicy Soy Sauce: Peel and halve 10 to 15 shallots and use in place of the scallions to produce a more substantial dish. Chopped leeks are also a good option.

| Add a tablespoon minced ginger and/or garlic to the simmering liquid during the last 5 minutes of cooking.

| Stir in a teaspoon wasabi paste (or to taste) just as the dish finishes cooking.

| Garnish with a small pile of shredded daikon radish.

Roast Salmon Steaks with Pinot Noir Syrup

TIME: 40 to 50 minutes
MAKES: 4 servings

I first had this mysterious, dark, extraordinarily delicious sauce at a Seattle restaurant called Brasa. It's a kind of *gastrique*, a relatively simple sauce that is based on caramelized sugar. Like many other foods—from coffee to bread to steak—sugar becomes somewhat bitter when browned, losing most if not all of its sweetness. In fact, it becomes markedly more complex, not only in flavor but in molecular structure. This considerable change is not routine in most kitchens, but it's pretty easy to produce (and if you fail, you've only lost a cup of sugar; try again, more slowly, and you'll get it).

½ cup sugar

2 cups Pinot Noir

1 sprig rosemary, plus 1 teaspoon chopped rosemary

4 salmon steaks, each about ½ pound

Salt and freshly ground black pepper

1 tablespoon balsamic vinegar

1 tablespoon butter

1 Preheat the oven to 450°F. Put the sugar in a heavy-bottomed saucepan, preferably nonstick and with rounded sides, and turn the heat to medium. Cook, without stirring (just shake the pan occasionally to redistribute the sugar) until the sugar liquefies and begins to turn brown, about 10 minutes. Turn off the heat, stand back, and carefully add the wine. Turn the heat to high and cook, stirring, until the caramel dissolves again. Then add the rosemary sprig and reduce over high heat, stirring occasionally, until the mixture is syrupy and reduced to just over ½ cup, 10 to 15 minutes.

2 Heat a nonstick skillet over high heat until it begins to smoke. Season the salmon on both sides with salt and pepper, then put it in the pan; immediately put the pan in the oven. Roast for 3 minutes, then turn the salmon and roast for another 3 minutes. Check to see that the salmon is medium-rare or thereabouts (it should be still orange in the center), remove it from the oven, and keep it warm, or cook for another 1 to 2 minutes if you like.

WINE Pinot Noir

SERVE WITH 60-Minute Bread (page 207) or good store-bought bread; Steamed Broccoli (or Other Vegetable) (page 203); Mashed Potatoes (page 205) or Crisp Potatoes (page 206)

3 When the sauce is reduced, stir in the balsamic vinegar and butter and turn the heat to medium-low. Cook until the butter melts. Add salt and pepper, and remove the rosemary sprig. Taste and adjust seasoning, then serve over the fish. Garnish with the chopped rosemary.

Keys To SUCCESS

IF THE SUGAR turns black and begins to smoke, you have burned rather than caramelized it. Throw it out and start again, with lower heat and more patience this time.

WHEN YOU'RE DONE, if the caramel sticks to your pan and utensils, boil some water in the pan, with the utensils in there if necessary. The caramel will loosen right away.

THE WINE YOU USE need not be expensive; as of this writing, Joseph Drouhin's La Forêt, sold for less than $12 a bottle, worked perfectly.

With MINIMAL Effort

The sauce seems best on salmon, where the flavors are complementary. Surprisingly enough, it's also good on cod, although the sauce dominates.

Roast Salmon with Spicy Soy Oil

It doesn't take much to cook salmon, or to dress it up, and there's no way simpler than this: Cook fillets by any of a number of methods, then finish them with flavored oil. Here I focus on a spicy soy oil that contains slivered garlic, peanut and sesame oils, and soy sauce, but it's easy enough to change the spirit from Asian to European. Although oil is the basis for this sauce, the quantity is minimal because heating the oil thins it, enabling even a small amount to coat and flavor the fish.

2 tablespoons peanut oil

1½ to 2 pounds salmon fillets, in 4 pieces

Salt and freshly ground black pepper

1 tablespoon toasted sesame oil

1 tablespoon slivered garlic

2 dried red chiles

1 tablespoon soy sauce

½ cup trimmed and chopped scallions or ¼ cup roughly chopped cilantro, optional

1 Preheat the oven to 500°F. Put a 12-inch nonstick oven-proof skillet over medium-high heat for 2 to 3 minutes. When it is hot, add 1 tablespoon of the peanut oil and swirl it around. Season the salmon with salt and pepper and put it, skin side up, in the skillet. Sear for 1 minute until the salmon has browned. Turn the salmon and immediately transfer the skillet to the oven. Roast for 6 minutes.

2 Meanwhile, combine the remaining 1 tablespoon peanut oil in a small saucepan with the sesame oil, garlic, and chiles and turn the heat to medium. Cook, gently shaking the pan occasionally, until the garlic and chiles sizzle and the garlic colors lightly, about 5 minutes. Turn off the heat and remove the chiles. (This step may be done in advance.) When the sauce cools a bit, add the soy sauce.

3 The salmon will be medium-rare after about 6 minutes in the oven. Transfer it to a plate. Drizzle it with the oil, garnish if you like, and serve.

WINE Beer is best, but with the European variations, a rough, rustic red from Chianti, southern France, or California is good.

SERVE WITH Easy Rice (page 204), Mashed Potatoes (page 205) or Crisp Potatoes (page 206); Steamed Broccoli (or Other Vegetable) (page 203); Simple Green Salad (page 196)

THE IDEAL piece of salmon is a 1½- to 2-inch-thick crosscut from the thick part of a fillet, weighing 6 to 8 ounces and serving one. Ask the fishmonger to cut a whole fillet in half and give you the thick end, which is of nearly uniform thickness. A piece that weighs 1½ to 2 pounds will make four servings, and you simply make the crosscuts yourself, at home.

SALMON IS almost always sold with the skin on, and the skin is good to eat, as long as it is scaled.

YOU CAN START the fish on top of the stove and finish it in the oven, a method that reduces stovetop spattering (and the airborne oils that stink up the kitchen), requires only one turn, and results in nicely browned pieces of fish. If you'd rather cook only on top of the stove, sear them for about 2 minutes on each of the skinless sides; after about 6 minutes, they'll be medium-rare and still orange in the center (cook for another couple of minutes if you prefer the fish better done). You can also roast them in a 450° to 500°F oven from start to finish (about 10 minutes total), or steam them on a rack or a plate (6 to 8 minutes total).

Salmon with Spicy Sherry Vinegar Oil: Cook the salmon exactly as above, using a total of 3 tablespoons of olive oil in place of the peanut and sesame oils. First, sear the salmon in 1 tablespoon of the olive oil, as above. Then combine the remaining 2 tablespoons olive oil in a small saucepan with the garlic, chiles, and some salt. Cook, gently shaking the pan occasionally, until the garlic and chiles sizzle and the garlic colors lightly, about 5 minutes. Turn off the heat and remove the chiles. (This step may be done in advance.) When the sauce cools a bit, add 1 tablespoon sherry vinegar. Garnish with ¼ cup roughly chopped parsley or 2 teaspoons minced fresh tarragon.

Salmon with Soy and Black Beans: Before cooking the fish, soak 1 tablespoon preserved (Chinese) black beans in 1 tablespoon dry sherry or water. Drain the beans and add them to the oil along with the garlic and chiles.

Salmon Roasted with Herbs

TIME: 20 to 30 minutes
MAKES: 4 servings

Although farm-raising has made fresh salmon a year-round product, wild salmon does have a season, from spring through fall. At those times, wild salmon is preferable to the farm-raised fish, because the best salmon—king, sockeye, and coho—have so much flavor of their own that they need nothing but a sprinkling of salt. But a simple formula of salmon, oil or butter, and a single herb, combined with a near-foolproof oven roasting technique, gives you many more options and makes even farm-raised salmon taste special.

¼ cup (½ stick) butter

¼ cup minced chervil, parsley, or dill

1 salmon fillet, 1½ to 2 pounds

Salt and freshly ground black pepper

Lemon wedges

1 Preheat the oven to 475°F. Place the butter and 2 tablespoons of the herbs in a roasting pan just large enough to fit the salmon (you may have to cut the fillet in half) and put it in the oven. Heat for about 5 minutes, until the butter melts and the herb begins to sizzle.

2 Add the salmon to the pan, skin side up. Roast for 4 minutes. Remove the pan from the oven, then remove the skin from the salmon (it should peel right off; if it does not, roast for another 2 minutes). Sprinkle with salt and pepper and turn the fillet. Sprinkle with salt and pepper again.

3 Roast for another 3 to 5 minutes, depending on the thickness of the fillet and degree of doneness you prefer. Spoon a little of the butter over each serving, garnish with the remaining 2 tablespoons herbs, and serve with lemon wedges.

WINE Red Burgundy, or Pinot Noir, full-bodied Chardonnay, or light red from the south of France, or even Chianti

SERVE WITH 60-Minute Bread (page 207) or good store-bought bread; Mashed Potatoes (page 205); Roasted Peppers (page 195) or Glazed Carrots (page 201)

BE SURE to preheat the pan in the oven—this allows the fish to brown before it overcooks. (If you start the same fillet in a cold pan, it will simply turn a dull pink, and will not brown until it is as dry as chalk.)

AFTER 3 OR 4 minutes in the oven, the salmon skin can be easily removed if you like. But as long as it has been scaled, the skin is good to eat.

Salmon Roasted in Olive Oil: Substitute extra virgin olive oil for the butter. Substitute basil, thyme leaves (2 teaspoons total), or marjoram (2 tablespoons total) for the chervil, parsley, or dill.

| Substitute peanut oil for the butter (adding a teaspoon toasted sesame oil for extra flavor if you like) and use cilantro or mint for the herb. Use limes instead of lemon.

Tuna or Swordfish with Onion Confit

TIME: 45 to 60 minutes

MAKES: 4 servings

Slow-cooked onions are good enough by themselves, but when you combine them with the liquid exuded by olives and tomatoes you have a gloriously juicy bed on which to serve any fish fillet or steak. This combination, I think, is best with grilled tuna or swordfish—their meatiness gives them the presence to stand up to the richly flavored mass of onions, creating an easy dish that has a Provençal feel and is perfect for summer.

3 tablespoons extra virgin olive oil

3 large or 4 to 5 medium onions, thinly sliced

Salt and freshly ground black pepper

1 large thyme sprig, or a large pinch of dried thyme

2 medium tomatoes

1½ to 2 pounds tuna or swordfish

About ½ cup roughly chopped good black olives

1 Pour the olive oil into a 10- or 12-inch skillet and turn the heat to medium. Add the onions, a healthy pinch of salt, some pepper, and the thyme. Cook, stirring occasionally, until the mixture starts to sizzle, a minute or two. Adjust the heat so that you only have to stir every 5 minutes at most to keep the onions from browning. They will become progressively softer; do not allow them to brown. Allow at least 30 minutes total for the onions to cook.

2 Meanwhile, core the tomatoes (cut a cone-shaped wedge out of the stem end), then cut them in half horizontally. Squeeze and shake out the seeds, then cut the tomatoes into ½-inch dice. Start a moderately hot charcoal or wood fire or preheat a gas grill to the maximum. Set the grilling rack about 4 inches from the heat source.

3 When the onions are very soft, almost a shapeless mass, season the fish with salt and pepper and grill it, turning once, for a total of about 6 minutes for tuna or 8 to 10 minutes for swordfish. Check for doneness by making a small cut in the center of the fish and peeking inside.

WINE Beaujolais, Chianti, or Zinfandel

SERVE WITH 60-Minute Bread (page 207) or good store-bought bread; Simple Green Salad (page 196) or Roasted Peppers (page 195)

(Tuna can be quite rare; swordfish is best cooked to medium, when its interior is still slightly pearly rather than completely opaque.) While the fish is grilling, stir the olives and tomatoes into the onions and raise the heat a bit; cook, stirring occasionally, until the tomatoes liquefy and the mixture becomes juicy, 5 to 10 minutes. Taste and adjust the seasoning. Serve the fish on a bed of the onion confit.

Chicken with Onion Confit: Serve the onions with grilled boneless chicken breasts.

| Omit the thyme and use a bay leaf instead, or finish the dish with a handful of chopped fresh basil, chervil, or parsley.

| Cook some finely chopped aromatic vegetables, like carrots, celery or fennel, and garlic, along with the onions.

Keys To SUCCESS

TO COOK ONIONS this way you must use a low flame and allow a fair amount of time, in this case about 30 to 40 minutes. During that time, the onions should not brown at all (or at the most, only slightly), and, for the first half of the cooking time, they should essentially be stewing in their own juices. Because the onions throw off so much liquid, you don't need much cooking fat.

THE TOMATOES can be skinned if you like, but I believe it's sufficient to core them, cut them in half horizontally, and shake out most of their seeds before dicing them.

Shad Roe with Mustard

Shad, the largest member of the herring family, migrates to the rivers of the East Coast every spring. It's a big, bony fish with moist flesh not unlike that of salmon. But its huge egg sacs, which come in pairs held together by a thin membrane, are the real attraction. They're filled with millions of eggs which, *if they are not overcooked*, remain creamy and rich in a way that is reminiscent of fine organ meat—not quite foie gras, but not that far away either. As a bonus, the exterior membrane becomes slightly crisp.

Like foie gras, shad roe is amazingly simple to cook and is rich, filling, and delicious. But unlike foie gras, it isn't all that expensive.

2 tablespoons butter

1 large pair shad roe, about 12 ounces

Salt and freshly ground black pepper

2 tablespoons Dijon mustard

Minced parsley, optional

1 Heat an 8- or 10-inch nonstick skillet over medium heat for a minute or two, then add the butter. When it melts, gently lay the shad roe in the pan and sprinkle it with salt and pepper. Cook for about 3 minutes, or until the underside is lightly browned.

2 Turn very gently—a large spatula is best for this—and season the cooked side. Cook for another 3 minutes or so, again until the underside is lightly browned. By this time the roe should be quite firm to the touch; if it is still soft, cover the pan and cook for another 1 to 2 minutes, then cut into it to check. When done, the center will be red and the area surrounding it pink.

3 Remove the roe to a warm plate and stir the mustard and ¼ cup of water into the pan. Raise the heat to high and stir the sauce with a wooden spoon until smooth and thick. Spoon over the roe, garnish with parsley if you like, and serve immediately.

WINE Red Burgundy, Pinot Noir, or something rough from southern France

SERVE WITH 60-Minute Bread (page 207) or good store-bought bread; Simple Green Salad (page 196)

USE A nonstick pan and sufficient butter to guarantee good flavor and a nicely browned crust.

KEEP THE cooking time short, just long enough to firm up the roe and cook it the equivalent of medium-rare. (It's okay to cut into it for a look-see the first couple of times you try this, but it's also pretty easy to get the hang of it, because the change in texture is rather dramatic.)

NOTE THAT this recipe serves two; it's easy enough to double, however. Use two pans if you must.

Shad Roe with Capers and Vinegar: In step 3, omit the mustard. Instead, stir in 2 tablespoons capers, a tablespoon sherry or other vinegar, and 2 tablespoons water. Stir until blended and the liquid reduced by about half. Spoon over the roe, garnish, and serve.

Shad Roe with Bacon: Omit the butter. Begin by cooking 4 thick slices of good bacon over medium heat until the fat is rendered and the bacon is done; remove the bacon and keep warm. Cook the shad roe in the bacon fat, exactly as above. Serve shad roe and bacon with lemon wedges, garnished with parsley.

SEARED AND STEAMED CHICKEN BREASTS

STEAMED CHICKEN BREASTS WITH SCALLION-GINGER SAUCE

FAST CHICKEN TANDOORI

CHICKEN CURRY WITH COCONUT MILK

CHICKEN BREAST WITH EGGPLANT, SHALLOTS, AND GINGER

CHICKEN-MUSHROOM "CUTLETS" WITH PARMESAN

CHICKEN WITH SORREL

SIMPLEST SAUTÉED CHICKEN WITH GARLIC

CHICKEN WITH APRICOTS

GRILLED CHICKEN THIGHS WITH SAUCE AU CHIEN

GRILLED CHICKEN WINGS WITH ANCHOVY DIPPING SAUCE

FASTEST ROAST CHICKEN

SOY-POACHED CHICKEN

Poultry

BROILED CORNISH HENS WITH LEMON AND BALSAMIC VINEGAR

ROASTED AND BRAISED DUCK WITH SAUERKRAUT

BAKED EGGS WITH ONIONS AND CHEESE

Seared and Steamed Chicken Breasts

TIME: 20 to 30 minutes

MAKES: 4 servings

Here's how to keep a boneless chicken breast moist while giving it a crust, and without using a lot of fat. This technique relies on two properties of the chicken breast that make it more like fish than like other meat. One, it cooks quickly. And two, it contains a fair amount of moisture. This enables you to start cooking the breasts with just a bit of fat over fairly high heat to begin browning, then lower the heat and cover the pan, which not only allows the meat to steam in its own juices but maintains the nicely browned exterior (on one side, anyway) and—a bonus that is certainly worth mentioning—reduces spattering to a minimum.

2 tablespoons extra virgin olive oil, butter, or a combination

4 plump boneless, skinless chicken breast halves (1½ to 2 pounds)

Salt and freshly ground black pepper

⅓ cup dry white wine, chicken stock, or water

1 cup peeled, seeded, and diced tomatoes (canned are fine; drain them first)

2 tablespoons capers

2 tablespoons chopped black olives, preferably imported

½ cup chopped fresh parsley leaves

1 Preheat the oven to 200°F. Pour the oil into a 12-inch skillet, turn the heat to medium-high, and heat for about 2 minutes. When the oil is hot, season the chicken breasts well with salt and pepper and place them in the skillet, smooth (skin) side down. Turn the heat to high and cook for about a minute, until the chicken begins to brown. Turn the heat to medium and cover the pan.

2 Cook, undisturbed, until the chicken is firm and nearly cooked through, 6 to 8 minutes. Uncover the skillet (there may be a little spattering from the moisture that has collected on the underside of the lid; removing the lid quickly will minimize this) and transfer the chicken to a plate; put the plate in the oven.

3 Over high heat, add the wine, stock, or water and stir and scrape to release any bits of chicken that have stuck to the bottom. When the liquid has reduced by about

WINE Light red, rosé, or crisp white, depending on your mood

SERVE WITH 60-Minute Bread (page 207) or good store-bought bread, Easy Rice (page 204), Mashed Potatoes (page 205), Crisp Potatoes (page 206), or almost any pasta dish; Simple Green Salad (page 196). It's hard to go wrong.

half, add the tomatoes and cook, stirring occasionally, for about a minute. Add the capers, olives, and all but 1 tablespoon of the parsley and cook for 1 minute more, stirring occasionally. Return the chicken to the sauce and turn once or twice. Sprinkle with the remaining 1 tablespoon parsley and serve.

Keys To SUCCESS

THE COOKING TIME for all but the thickest chicken breasts prepared this way is under 10 minutes; don't overcook them or the meat will become tough.

IF YOU USE mass-produced commercial chicken the results will be somewhat cottony. Free-range or kosher chickens are generally somewhat better.

With MINIMAL Effort

| Before adding the liquid in step 3, sauté a bit of chopped onion, shallot, mushroom, or other vegetables in the pan; proceed as above, with or without the tomatoes, capers, and olives.

| For the wine or stock, substitute cream.

| Use chopped basil or a few thyme leaves in place of the parsley.

| This simple technique will work perfectly well with most fish fillets or steaks, from salmon to cod to striped bass. Cooking time for most cuts of these fish will be just a little bit less than that for chicken breasts.

Steamed Chicken Breasts with Scallion-Ginger Sauce

TIME: 20 to 30 minutes
MAKES: 4 servings

Occasionally, I stumble over a culinary combination so obvious that I don't know whether to marvel over the bad luck that has kept it from me until now or the good luck that finally brought it my way. This was certainly the case with the Chinese dipping sauce of oil, scallions, ginger, and salt that I had in a Cantonese restaurant in Vancouver. It was served with chicken that had been steamed, then lightly dressed with soy and sesame oil; but my host demonstrated the usefulness of the sauce by stirring it into soup as well.

To make this sauce, you do nothing more than mince ginger and combine it with chopped scallions, oil, and plenty of salt.

- 4 chicken breast halves, bone-in or out (see Keys to Success)
- 1 tablespoon minced ginger
- ½ cup grapeseed, corn, or other light oil
- ¼ cup trimmed and chopped scallions, white and green parts combined (¼-inch pieces)
- Salt
- 2 tablespoons good soy sauce
- 1 teaspoon toasted sesame oil

1 Steam the chicken over simmering water for 6 to 10 minutes for boneless breasts, 10 to 15 minutes for bone-in. The chicken is done when white and firm to the touch; cut into a piece if you want to be certain.

2 Meanwhile, stir together the ginger, oil, scallions, and salt to taste in a bowl. The mixture should be quite strong; you can add more ginger, scallions, or salt if you like.

3 When the chicken is done, drizzle it with the soy sauce and sesame oil and serve. Pass the scallion-ginger sauce at the table or divide it into four small bowls for dipping.

WINE Beer, or a light, crisp white, like Sauvignon Blanc, Graves, Pinot Grigio, Pinot Gris, or dry Pinot Blanc

SERVE WITH Easy Rice (page 204) or Rice Salad with Peas and Soy (page 200); Green Salad with Soy Vinaigrette (page 197) or Steamed Broccoli (or Other Vegetable) (page 203) drizzled with a little soy sauce

YOU CAN speed up production by puréeing the ginger and oil in a blender, then pulsing in the scallion, but this makes the sauce creamy, almost muddy, and it's much more attractive when hand-chopped, the solids sitting in the oil.

I LIKE to steam the breasts on the bone, which takes about 5 minutes longer than boneless breasts, because they remain moister and a little more flavorful that way, but of course you can use boneless breasts. I also like to leave the skin on, which insulates the meat from drying out; again, you can use breasts that have had the skin removed.

IF YOU don't have a steamer, here's how to jury-rig one: Put a rack into a pan and add water to a level just shy of the bottom of the rack. The chicken can go directly on the rack or on a plate on the rack. Cover the pan while cooking.

MAKE SURE your oil is fresh; if it smells off, it is.

| This is a powerful sauce, one that will markedly change the character of anything to which you add it. Stir it into soup, noodles, or simply a bowl of rice, or steam some fish—just as you would chicken—and serve the sauce with that.

Fast Chicken Tandoori

TIME: 20 minutes or more

MAKES: 4 servings

There are two ways to think of chicken tandoori. Strictly defined, it is yogurt-marinated chicken cooked in a *tandoor*, a clay oven of central Asian origin that is closely associated with Indian cooking and often used to bake bread. But you can also think of chicken tandoori as grilled or broiled chicken marinated in yogurt and spices. That's what we have here—a lightning-quick, really easy tandoori-style dish that begins with a boneless, skinless chicken breast and "marinates" for just a few minutes.

1 cup plain yogurt

1 teaspoon minced ginger

1 teaspoon minced garlic

1 teaspoon medium-to-hot paprika

1 teaspoon ground coriander

Juice of 1 lime

Salt and freshly ground black pepper

1½ pounds boneless, skinless chicken breasts

Minced fresh cilantro

1 Preheat the broiler, start a hot charcoal or wood fire, or preheat a gas grill to the maximum. Set the rack 2 to 4 inches from the heat source. Combine the yogurt, ginger, garlic, paprika, half the lime juice, and some salt and pepper in a large bowl. Stir the chicken into the yogurt mixture and marinate for 5 to 60 minutes, as time allows.

2 TO BROIL THE CHICKEN, line a baking sheet with aluminum foil to facilitate cleanup. To broil, put the chicken breasts on the baking sheet, bone (rough) side up; reserve any marinade that does not cling to the breasts. Broil for 3 to 4 minutes, or until lightly browned. Turn and spoon the remaining marinade over the chicken. Broil on the skin (smooth) side for another 3 to 4 minutes, or until lightly browned.

TO GRILL THE CHICKEN, simply grill for 3 to 4 minutes per side, or until the chicken browns and is cooked through, brushing with the marinade from time to time.

3 Garnish with cilantro and serve, spooning the basting juices over the chicken.

WINE Spicy, light red, like Zinfandel, Chianti, or Côtes du Rhône

SERVE WITH Easy Rice (page 204), rice pilaf, or Indian-style bread; Simple Green Salad (page 196)

FOR THE SAKE of speed, the chicken can sit in the yogurt mixture for as little as 5 minutes, but a soak of about an hour allows a little more of the flavor to permeate the flesh. After a few hours, however, the meat just begins to become mushy in texture.

| The yogurt mixture is so creamy and delicious that, even in grilling season, I like to double the quantity and broil the chicken, so I can use the cooked sauce and meat drippings to top cooked rice.

Chicken Curry with Coconut Milk

Coconut milk could hardly be easier to use. Like canned tomatoes, it is the foundation of certain essential dishes, especially those of India, Southeast Asia, and the Caribbean. Like canned chicken stock, it can turn a dry dish into a pleasantly saucy one in about 2 minutes. Like both, it can be always there for you, since it is also sold in cans. This dish, a simple, fast curry, is made sweet and creamy by nothing more than the addition of coconut milk; it's a snap.

2 tablespoons vegetable oil

2 large onions, sliced

Salt and freshly ground black pepper

2 teaspoons curry powder

One 12- to 14-ounce can (1½ to 2 cups) unsweetened coconut milk

1½ pounds boneless, skinless chicken, cut into ¾- to 1-inch chunks

1 cup peeled, seeded, and diced tomato (canned is fine; cut up and drain before using)

Chopped fresh basil or mint

1 Pour the oil into a large skillet, turn the heat to medium-high, and heat for a minute. Add the onions, along with a generous pinch of salt and some pepper. Reduce the heat to medium and cook, stirring occasionally, until the onions are very soft and almost falling apart, 15 minutes or more. Raise the heat again and brown them a bit, then stir in the curry powder and cook, stirring, for another minute or so.

2 Reduce the heat to medium, add the coconut milk, and cook, stirring occasionally, until it thickens, about 2 minutes. Add the chicken and stir, then cook until done, 3 to 6 minutes. (If you're in doubt whether the chicken is done, cut into a piece.)

3 Add the tomato and cook for another minute; taste and adjust the seasoning as necessary. Garnish with basil and serve.

WINE Dry Riesling or Gewürztraminer or beer

SERVE WITH Easy Rice (page 204) or any rice dish; Green Salad with Soy Vinaigrette (page 197) or any light salad

TO MAKE YOUR OWN coconut milk, combine 2 cups grated unsweetened coconut and 2 cups boiling water in a blender; let cool a bit, then blend carefully, taking care that the hot liquid does not splatter. Strain and discard solids.

| For the chicken, substitute peeled shrimp or scallops; the cooking time will be a little bit shorter, though not much. Scallops would be decidedly better if you sear them in a very hot pan before adding them to the curry.

Chicken Breast with Eggplant, Shallots, and Ginger

TIME: 30 to 40 minutes
MAKES: 4 servings

Eggplant is so strongly associated with the cooking of Italy and southern France that regardless of cooking method it is almost always prepared with olive oil and garlic. This need not be the case, of course, and with a few ingredient changes—like the addition of ginger—you can make a novel and delicious kind of "ratatouille" that readily converts an ordinary grilled or broiled boneless chicken breast into an unusual and appealing dish.

8 ounces shallots (about 6 large)

¼ cup grapeseed, corn, or other light oil

1 to 1¼ pounds eggplant, cut into 1-inch cubes

Salt and freshly ground black pepper

2 tablespoons minced fresh ginger, or 2 teaspoons dried

1½ pounds boneless, skinless, chicken breasts (4 half breasts)

¼ cup or more minced fresh cilantro

1 Peel the shallots and cut them in half the long way (most large shallots have two lobes anyway, and will naturally divide in half as you peel them). If they are small, peel them and leave them whole. Start a medium hot charcoal or wood fire, preheat a gas grill to the maximum, or preheat the broiler. Set the rack 4 inches above the heat source.

2 Pour the oil into a large, nonstick skillet and turn the heat to medium-high. Add the shallots and cook for about 5 minutes, stirring occasionally, until they begin to brown. Add the eggplant, salt, and pepper and lower the heat to medium. Cook, stirring occasionally, until the eggplant softens, about 15 minutes.

3 When the eggplant begins to brown, add the ginger and cook for another 3 minutes or so, until the eggplant is very tender and the mixture fragrant. Meanwhile, rub the chicken breasts with salt, pepper, and 1 tablespoon of the ginger. Grill or broil for 3 minutes per side, or until done.

WINE Rough red from the south of France, Zinfandel, Syrah, or Chianti

SERVE WITH 60-Minute Bread (page 207) or good store-bought bread; boiled or Mashed Potatoes (page 205) or Easy Rice (page 204)

4 Stir 2 tablespoons of the cilantro into the eggplant mixture. Serve the chicken breasts on a bed of the eggplant and garnish with the remaining 2 tablespoons cilantro.

Keys To SUCCESS

UNLESS YOU HAVE reason to believe that your eggplant is extremely bitter (if it has a lot of seeds it might be), don't bother to salt it. If you choose to, sprinkle the cubes liberally with salt and let them sit in a colander for at least 30 minutes. Rinse and dry before proceeding.

IDEALLY, this dish combines creamy eggplant with tender but ever-so-slightly crunchy shallots and ginger that hasn't lost its sharpness. So be sure to spend a few minutes thoroughly cooking the shallots before adding the eggplant, allowing them to brown and begin to soften; and don't overcook the ginger.

With MINIMAL Effort

| For a more traditional dish, substitute garlic for the ginger (or use 1 tablespoon of each) and cook in olive oil. Use parsley in place of cilantro.

| Stir in a cup or more of seeded and chopped tomatoes at the last minute; these boost color as well as flavor, and the combination of tomatoes and ginger is another unexpectedly pleasant one. (Peel the tomatoes if you like, but I don't think it's worth the effort in this case.)

| Cook some chopped red or yellow bell pepper along with the eggplant.

| Use any reasonably tender steak of beef, pork, or lamb, or a sturdy piece of fish, such as tuna or swordfish, instead of the chicken.

Chicken-Mushroom "Cutlets" with Parmesan

TIME: 20 to 30 minutes

MAKES: 4 servings

I call these "cutlets," though they are in fact burgers. But calling something a chickenburger might make it sound like a 50s throwback or an unappealing fast-food offering. Still, if you produce such an item with up-to-the minute ingredients, the taste is undeniably fine, far better than any other burger alternative I've come across. Leave out the filler and skip the bun, and it becomes nearly pure protein and very contemporary.

1 ounce dried porcini or shiitake mushrooms

4 ounces Parmigiano-Reggiano (about 1 cup grated)

2 garlic cloves, peeled

1 teaspoon freshly ground black pepper

Pinch salt

1½ pounds boneless, skinless chicken or turkey breasts, cut into large chunks

2 tablespoons extra virgin olive oil

1 Put the dried mushrooms in a bowl and cover with hot water.

2 Cut the cheese into chunks and put it in the container of a food processor along with the garlic; process until well grated. (If the cheese is already grated, just pulse the machine on and off a couple of times.)

3 Add the pepper, salt, and chicken and pulse the machine on and off until the chicken is chopped, not puréed. Squeeze the excess water from the mushrooms but do not wring them completely dry. Add them to the machine and pulse 2 or 3 more times, until the mixture is more-or-less combined but, again, not pureed.

4 Put the olive oil in a 12-inch nonstick skillet and turn the heat to medium. Shape the chicken mixture into eight small burger-shaped cakes. Cook for about 3 minutes per side, or until nicely browned. Do not overcook; when the cutlets are firm, they are done. Serve hot or at room temperature, with any condiment you like.

WINE Beaujolais, Zinfandel, inexpensive Pinot Noir, Chianti, or any lively red

SERVE WITH 60-Minute Bread (page 207) or store-bought bread, or hamburger buns and ketchup; Simple Green Salad (page 196) or any salad

TAKE CARE in preparing these: The chicken must be chopped, not puréed; too fine a texture will create a dense, almost impenetrable patty. This can be done in the food processor as long as you pay attention and don't overprocess.

THE MEAT must be cooked through, but must not be overcooked or it will become tough and dry; when the burger feels firm to the touch, it's done.

| Grill these if you like, or cook them in butter instead of olive oil.

| Add a teaspoon or so of minced garlic or ginger to the seasoning mix.

| Substitute a fistful of cooked, squeezed-nearly-dry spinach for the mushrooms, or add about ¼ cup chopped parsley or other herb to the food processor along with the chicken.

| Substitute pork, beef, veal, or a combination for the chicken.

Chicken
with Sorrel

A leafy green that looks something like flat-leaf spinach, sorrel is also known as sour grass, which deftly describes its flavor. Its tendency practically to liquefy when cooked has determined its destiny, usually as an ingredient in sauces or in an Eastern European soup called schav. This rare capacity to create a sauce simply by being cooked, while adding a creamy texture and lemony flavor, makes it a natural if unusual partner for braised chicken.

2 tablespoons unsalted butter or extra virgin olive oil

One 2½- to 3-pound chicken, cut into serving pieces

Salt and freshly ground black pepper

1 large or 2 medium onions, sliced ¼ inch thick

6 cups sorrel (about ½ pound), trimmed and washed

1 Put the butter in a large skillet, preferably nonstick, and turn the heat to medium-high. When the butter begins to melt, swirl it around the pan; when its foam subsides and it begins to brown, add the chicken, skin side down. Cook, rotating the pieces after 3 or 4 minutes so they brown evenly. As they brown on the skin side, sprinkle them with salt and pepper and turn them over; sprinkle the skin side, now on top, with salt and pepper as well. If at any point it becomes necessary to prevent burning, lower the heat to medium. When the chicken is completely browned all over, which will take 10 to 15 minutes, transfer it to a plate.

2 Immediately add the onions to the skillet and cook, stirring occasionally, until they begin to soften but still hold their shape, just 5 minutes or so. Add ½ cup water and cook for a minute, stirring occasionally, until it reduces slightly. Return the chicken to the pan, turn the heat to medium-low, and cook, covered, for about 10 minutes. Uncover, add the sorrel, stir, and cover again.

3 Cook for about 10 minutes longer, uncovering and stirring occasionally, until the chicken is cooked through and the sorrel dissolved into the onions and liquid. Taste, adjust the seasoning if necessary, and serve.

WINE California Chardonnay

SERVE WITH 60-Minute Bread (page 207) or good store-bought bread; Easy Rice (page 204); Glazed Carrots (page 201)

SORREL IS a perennial that survives northeastern winters and is in season most of the summer. You can buy it at many greenmarkets and farm stands, at good food stores, and at some supermarkets. It is usually sold in small bunches. Wash it well to remove all traces of grit before using.

SPINACH IS close to sorrel in many ways, and although it won't fall apart as sorrel does in a sauce, its astringency makes it the best substitute in this recipe.

| After the sorrel has dissolved, remove the chicken and stir ½ to 1 cup cream or sour cream into the sauce.

Simplest Sautéed Chicken with Garlic

TIME: 30 to 40 minutes
MAKES: 4 servings

Sautéed chicken should be crisp, moist, and flavorful, and you can accomplish this easily. But like many dishes with few ingredients, one requirement is quite specific: You need a good chicken—this is not the place for the cotton-textured, mass-produced birds. My personal preference is for kosher chicken, but that may be because for me the paradigm of pan-cooked chicken is my maternal grandmother's, and she kept a kosher home. You might choose a free-range bird instead, which has a similar taste and texture.

1 small chicken (2 to 3 pounds), cut into serving pieces

Salt and freshly ground black pepper

½ teaspoon sweet paprika

1 teaspoon minced garlic

Chopped parsley, optional

Lemon wedges, optional

1 Put the chicken skin side down in a nonstick skillet large enough to comfortably accommodate it without crowding; use two skillets if necessary. Turn the heat to medium and season with salt and pepper. About 5 minutes after the chicken begins to make cooking noises, peek at the underside of the pieces. If they are browning evenly, leave them alone; but if some adjusting of heat or shifting of the parts is necessary to accomplish even browning, do it. Don't turn any piece until it is evenly golden-brown on the first side—not very dark, but crisp-looking—then turn them as they're ready. It should take about 10 minutes to brown on the first side.

2 Season the skin, now up, with salt, pepper, and paprika. Cook the second side as you did the first; when it is nearly done, add the garlic to the skillet. As the pieces finish browning, turn them skin side down once again.

3 Continue to cook, turning once or twice more if necessary, until the pieces are done (if you have any doubts, cut into a piece or two; there should be no traces of red blood, but some pinkness is okay). Breast pieces will undoubtedly finish first; you can keep them warm in a low oven or just serve them less than piping hot. When the chicken is ready, garnish with parsley and lemon wedges if you like, and serve.

WINE Light or even full-bodied red, from Beaujolais to Burgundy

SERVE WITH Roasted or baked potatoes; Simple Green Salad (page 196); Steamed Broccoli (or Other Vegetable) (page 203) or Glazed Carrots (page 201)

USE A LARGE SKILLET, or two smaller ones, because crowding the chicken pieces prevents them from browning. There should be sufficient room in the skillet so that the pieces barely touch each other, and they should certainly not overlap.

BECAUSE THIS RECIPE contains no added fat—the bird provides plenty of its own—the skillet should be non-stick, or at least very well seasoned.

THIS PREPARATION is far from difficult, but it does require attention. If the heat is too high, the chicken will scorch and dry out; if it is too low, the chicken will become soggy and never brown.

| A mild, high-quality chile powder, like that made from ground ancho peppers, provides a more distinctive taste than paprika.

| Other spices, or a spice mix, are also good—curry powder; five-spice powder; a mixture of cinnamon, allspice, and a pinch of ground cloves, for example—but in similarly small amounts.

| For the garlic, substitute ginger, scallions, onions, or shallots.

Chicken with Apricots

TIME: 40 to 50 minutes
MAKES: 4 servings

Chicken with dried apricots is hardly a new idea, but it's almost always too sweet, and the routine addition of cinnamon and cloves makes the whole thing taste more like dessert than dinner. Take them away, add a little vinegar to counter the fruit's sweetness, improve and simplify the cooking technique, and you have an attractive dish for a winter meal.

1 cup dried apricots or other dried fruit

¼ cup red wine vinegar

½ cup fruity red wine

1 chicken, about 3 pounds, cut into serving pieces

Salt and freshly ground black pepper

1 medium onion, chopped

1 Put the apricots in a small bowl (or a 2-cup measure) and add the vinegar, wine, and water to cover, about ¼ cup. Let soak while you brown the chicken.

2 Turn the heat to medium-high under a 12-inch nonstick skillet and add the chicken, skin side down. Cook, rotating the pieces (not turning them) so they brown evenly. When they are nicely browned—10 to 15 minutes—turn them so they are skin side up, and season with salt and pepper. Make a little space in which you can add the onion and cook, stirring the onion occasionally, until it has softened a bit, 1 to 2 minutes.

3 Add the apricots and their liquid and bring to a boil. Cook for a minute, then turn the heat to low, and cover. Cook until the chicken is done, 15 to 20 minutes; do not turn while it is cooking. Remove the lid, raise the heat, and season the chicken well with salt and pepper. Boil out any excess liquid; you do not want the sauce to be too watery. Taste and adjust the seasoning if necessary, and serve.

WINE Rioja or another rich, soft red

SERVE WITH 60-Minute Bread (page 207) or good store-bought bread; Easy Rice (page 204) or any other grain; Crisp Potatoes (page 206); Steamed Broccoli (or Other Vegetable) (page 203)

HERE, THE CHICKEN is carefully browned, then turned skin-side up and braised in the apricots and the liquid. Do not turn it again, so the skin remains nicely browned and even a little crisp, rather than becoming mushy.

FRUIT THAT HAS been dried with sulfur—the most common method—is moister and much faster to tenderize than fruit dried organically, which will need at least a couple of hours of soaking before cooking.

| A few sprigs of fresh thyme add another dimension to this dish.

| A tablespoon or two of butter, stirred in at the end, will make the sauce considerably richer. Or you might render some bacon, remove it, and brown the chicken in the bacon fat; crumble the bacon and stir it in at the end of cooking.

| Use any dried fruit you like, or a combination; with such a short cooking time, even prunes will remain intact.

Grilled Chicken Thighs with Sauce au Chien

TIME: 30 minutes (longer, if grilling)
MAKES: 4 servings

Once in Martinique I ate at a restaurant with a menu so simple almost all of the food—chicken, tuna, quail, pork, and veal kidneys—was grilled. Everything was served with the same thin, powerful sauce, made of lime, scallion, chile, garlic, and loads of allspice. It was the allspice that made the sauce unusual, but there was more to it than that: The garlic and scallions looked uncooked but had lost their harshness and become easily digestible in a water base. With the help of a friend who was born on Martinique, I was able to duplicate the sauce at home. It's called "sauce au chien," which means "dog sauce" (a fact I chose not to research too aggressively). And it's great with almost anything grilled.

1 tablespoon slivered or minced garlic

6 scallions, trimmed and minced

1 jalapeño, habanero, or Scotch bonnet pepper, stemmed, seeded, and minced, or Asian chili paste or crushed red pepper flakes to taste (start with about ½ teaspoon)

Salt and freshly ground black pepper

½ teaspoon ground allspice, or to taste

1 tablespoon peanut, or grapeseed, corn, or other light oil

8 chicken thighs (about 2 pounds)

Juice of 1 lime

1 Start a charcoal or wood fire, or preheat a gas grill to the maximum, or preheat the broiler. Set the rack about 6 inches from the heat source. Meanwhile, prepare the sauce: Combine the garlic, scallions, chile, ½ teaspoon each of salt and pepper, allspice, and oil in a small bowl. Add ½ cup boiling water; stir and let sit.

2 Sprinkle the chicken with salt and pepper and grill or broil it, turning two or three times, until it is cooked through, about 15 minutes. Taste the sauce and add more chile, salt, pepper, or allspice if needed. Stir in the lime juice. Serve the chicken hot or at room temperature, passing the sauce at the table.

WINE Rough, no-name red from Bordeaux, the south of France, or almost anywhere in Italy

SERVE WITH Coconut Rice and Beans (page 211) and perhaps some sliced cucumbers with sauce au chien drizzled over them

THE TAMING of the strong spices is achieved by pouring boiling water over the solid ingredients; the lime juice must be added at the last moment in order for it to retain its freshness.

SCOTCH BONNET pepper, with its fierce heat and distinctive flavor, makes this sauce more authentic. But a small amount of Asian chili paste is fine, as is any other source of heat.

IF YOU HAVE the patience to mince or grind allspice berries, the sauce will taste brighter; preground allspice will do the trick, as long as it is reasonably fresh.

| Serve the sauce with grilled fish or shellfish (especially shrimp), grilled ribs, or in fact, grilled pork of any kind, or any grilled poultry.

| Add some chopped capers to the finished sauce to vary the flavor.

Grilled Chicken Wings with Anchovy Dipping Sauce

TIME: 30 minutes (longer, if grilling)
MAKES: 4 servings

Properly grilled chicken is a pleasure, even when you dress it with nothing but lemon juice—or even salt. But if you make this Ligurian-inspired full-flavored dipping sauce based on anchovies, you can turn the simple grilled chicken into something really special. And the sauce can be used for whatever else you're serving at the same time.

3 pounds chicken wings

Salt and freshly ground black pepper

3 tablespoons extra virgin olive oil

3 tablespoons butter (or use 6 tablespoons oil total)

2 garlic cloves, roughly chopped

10 oil-packed anchovy fillets, or to taste, plus some of their oil

1 Preheat the broiler; or start a charcoal or gas grill; in either case, the fire should not be too hot and the rack should be 4 to 6 inches from the heat source. If you like, cut the chicken wings at each of their two joints to make three pieces and discard the tips (or save for stock); you can also cook the wings whole.

2 Grill or broil the wings, turning frequently, until thoroughly cooked and nicely browned. As they are cooking, sprinkle them with a little salt and a lot of pepper.

3 Meanwhile, combine the oil and butter in a small saucepan and turn the heat to low. When the butter melts, add the garlic and anchovies. Cook, stirring occasionally, until the anchovies break up and the sauce bubbles. Add salt if necessary and a good sprinkling of black pepper.

4 Serve the chicken hot or at room temperature, with the hot sauce for dipping or drizzling.

WINE Light, fruity red with guts, like Zinfandel, or something from the south of France, or Chianti

SERVE WITH 60-Minute Bread (page 207) or good store-bought bread; Easy Rice (page 204); cooked or raw vegetables, dipped in this same sauce

WHEN YOU'RE grilling chicken, don't build too hot a fire, and keep part of the grill cool—don't put any fuel under it at all—so you can move the pieces over to it in the (likely) event of flare-ups.

BROIL THE CHICKEN if you prefer; adjust the broiling rack so that it is 4 to 6 inches from the heat source, and turn the meat as it browns.

| This sauce makes a great dressing for grilled fish as well. It's also good with raw or lightly cooked vegetables.

| Chicken thighs, or leg-thigh pieces, are just as good as wings here; the cooking time will be a little longer.

Fastest Roast Chicken

TIME: 45 to 60 minutes
MAKES: 4 servings

Roast chicken is one of the most basic dishes of home cooking, but there are a couple of challenges: You need high heat to brown the skin, but ultra-high heat may burn it. You need to cook the legs through before the more delicate breast dries out. And, if you're interested in minimalist cooking, you must accomplish these things without a lot of fuss, such as turning the chicken over three times, searing it on top of the stove before roasting, or constantly adjusting the oven temperature. Plus, you want to do it all as fast as possible. Well, here it is: fast, nearly foolproof roast chicken.

1 whole chicken (3 to 4 pounds)

Salt and freshly ground black pepper

1 Preheat the oven to 450°F. Five minutes after turning on the oven, place a cast-iron or other heavy, ovenproof skillet on a rack set low in the oven. (Alternatively, put the skillet over high heat about 3 minutes before the oven is hot.) Season the chicken with salt and pepper.

2 When the oven is hot, about 10 minutes later, carefully place the chicken, breast side up, in the hot skillet. Roast, undisturbed, for 30 minutes, or until an instant-read thermometer inserted in the meaty part of the thigh registers 155°F. Remove from the oven, let rest for a minute or two, then carve and serve.

WINE The best red you can lay your hands on
SERVE WITH 60-Minute Bread (page 207) or good store-bought bread; Mashed Potatoes (page 205); Steamed Broccoli (or Other Vegetable) (page 203); Glazed Carrots (page 201)

THE KEY is to start the chicken in a hot skillet—cast iron is best—and put it in a very hot oven. Preheating the pan gets the bottom of the bird cooking first and fastest. And, quite fortuitously, that's the part—the meaty thigh—that takes the longest to cook.

YOU CAN start preheating the skillet on top of the stove if you prefer that to the oven, and it has one advantage: You can get the pan blazing hot, and it's marginally easier to put the chicken into it. But be aware that putting a chicken in a hot skillet will produce volumes of smoke almost instantly—you'll want to get that skillet into the oven right away.

| To make a quick gravy while the chicken is resting, pour out most of the fat, put the skillet over high heat, and add about a cup of water, wine, or stock. Cook, stirring and scraping, until just about ½ cup liquid is left. Season with salt and pepper and, if you're feeling extravagant, a tablespoon or two of butter.

| Rub the chicken with olive oil and/or any herbs you like about halfway through the cooking—especially good is a bit of tarragon or a mixture of chopped rosemary and garlic.

Soy-Poached Chicken

TIME: 40 to 60 minutes

MAKES: 4 servings

My friend Roy Ip grew up eating chicken poached in soy sauce, a traditional Chinese dish I always liked, so I got him to show me how to make it. The preparation is simple: You boil the soy and wine along with some water, ginger, and crushed sugar, adding star anise, ginger, and scallion for flavor. The chicken is boiled too—not simmered, really boiled—but only for 10 minutes; it finishes cooking in the liquid with the heat turned off.

3 cups mushroom-flavored soy sauce, or any dark soy sauce

3 cups (one bottle) mei kuei lu chiew wine, or any floral, off-dry white wine, like Gewürztraminer or Muscat

2 pieces star anise

14 ounces yellow rock sugar (1 box), or 1 cup white sugar

3 ounces ginger (about a 5-inch knob), cut into thick slices and bruised with the side of a knife

10 medium scallions, untrimmed

1 whole chicken (2½ to 3 pounds)

1 In a narrow pot with about a 6-quart capacity, combine the soy sauce, wine, 2 cups water, and star anise over high heat. While the sugar is still in its box (or wrapped in a towel), smack it several times with a hammer or rolling pin to break it up; it need not be too fine. Add the sugar and ginger to the liquid and bring it to a rolling boil.

2 Add 6 of the scallions, then gently and slowly lower the chicken into the liquid, breast side down. (In a narrow pot, the liquid will easily cover the chicken; if it is close, just dunk the chicken under the liquid as it cooks. If it is not close, add a mixture of equal parts of soy sauce and water to raise the level.) Bring the liquid back to a boil and boil steadily for 10 minutes. Turn off the heat and turn the chicken over so the breast side is up. Let it sit in the hot liquid for 15 minutes. Meanwhile, trim and mince the remaining 4 scallions and preheat the oven to 500°F, if you like.

WINE Beer, Gewürztraminer, or Riesling

SERVE WITH Easy Rice (page 204) or Crisp Pan-Fried Noodle Cake (page 212); Steamed Broccoli (or Other Vegetable) (page 203)

3 Carefully remove the chicken from the liquid and serve it, hot or at room temperature. Or place it in a skillet or roasting pan. Roast for 5 minutes, or until nicely browned; keep an eye on it, because it can burn easily. In either case, reheat the sauce and, when the chicken is ready, carve it. Serve the chicken with a few spoonfuls of sauce on it. Pour another cup or so of the sauce in a bowl and add the minced scallions; pass this at the table.

Keys To SUCCESS

THERE ARE UNUSUAL but inexpensive ingredients that make this dish slightly better: mushroom-flavored soy sauce, which is dark and heavy; yellow rock sugar, a not-especially-sweet, lumpy sugar that must be broken up with a hammer before using; and mei kuei lu chiew, or "rose wine," a floral wine that smells like rosewater and costs 2 bucks a bottle. But don't knock yourself out looking for any of these. I give substitutes in the recipe.

THE TRADITIONAL METHOD is to remove the bird from the liquid and serve it without further cooking, hot or at room temperature. I like to brown it, by removing the chicken from the liquid and placing it in a hot oven where, in just 5 minutes, it develops a dark brown, crispy crust; this browning can also be done a few hours later.

PERHAPS THE BEST thing about this sauce is that it can be used time and again, as long as you freeze it between uses (or refrigerate it and bring it to a rolling boil every few days), and top up the liquids now and then.

With MINIMAL Effort

| Poach other vegetables in the soy sauce mixture for added flavor, and to serve along with the chicken. Root vegetables, such as carrots, turnips, and parsnips, are best

| Cook cut-up chicken or Cornish hens in the same way; the cooking time will be somewhat less

Broiled Cornish Hens with Lemon and Balsamic Vinegar

TIME: 30 to 40 minutes
MAKES: 4 servings

All sourness is not the same, as this simple preparation of broiled Cornish hens with lemon and vinegar demonstrates. I wanted to develop a dish that would take advantage of the complex flavor of the entire lemon, rind and all, and offset it with another equally gentle sourness.

The result is a crisp-skinned Cornish hen (you could use chicken, of course), topped with nicely browned lemon slices (sweet and tender enough to eat) and drizzled with just enough balsamic vinegar to make you wonder where the extra flavor is coming from. A garnish of parsley or a hint of rosemary and garlic make nice additions.

2 Cornish hens or 1 chicken
Salt and freshly ground black pepper
2 lemons
2 teaspoons balsamic vinegar, or to taste
Chopped parsley for garnish

1 Preheat the broiler and adjust the rack so that it is about 4 inches from the heat source. Use a sharp, sturdy knife to split the hens through their backbones; it will cut through without too much effort. Flatten the hens in a broiling or roasting pan, skin side down, and liberally sprinkle the exposed surfaces with salt and pepper. Slice one of the lemons as thinly as you can and lay the slices on the birds.

2 Broil for about 10 minutes, or until the lemon is browned and the birds appear cooked on this side; rotate the pan in the oven if necessary. Turn the birds, sprinkle with salt and pepper, and return to the broiler. Cook for another 10 minutes, or until the skin of the birds is nicely browned. Meanwhile, slice the remaining lemon as you did the first.

3 Lay the lemon slices on the birds' skin side and return to the broiler. Broil for another 5 minutes, by which time the lemons will be slightly browned and the meat cooked through; if it isn't, broil for an additional couple of minutes. Drizzle with the balsamic vinegar, garnish with parsley, and serve.

WINE Rosé from Provence or the Rhône, lightly chilled, or a light red like a Beaujolais

SERVE WITH 60-Minute Bread (page 207) or good store-bought bread; Easy Rice (page 204) or Mashed Potatoes (page 205); Sautéed Shiitake Mushrooms (page 202) or Steamed Broccoli (or Other Vegetable) (page 203)

A MANDOLINE is the tool of choice for slicing the lemons. (The inexpensive plastic mandolines made in Japan are among the most valuable kitchen gadgets.)

ADJUST THE DISTANCE between the rack and the heat source so the birds brown slowly but steadily. In my oven, a 4-inch gap is perfect for Cornish hens, but I must move it down to the next level for chickens, which take a little longer. If you have an electric oven, chances are the heating element will cycle off when the oven becomes hot; you can counter this by leaving the over door a little bit ajar while you're cooking, and moving the bird as far back in the oven as possible.

In step 3, spread 1 teaspoon finely minced garlic combined with 1 tablespoon minced fresh rosemary (or 1 teaspoon dried) on the birds' skin after it browns but before covering with the lemon slices.

Roasted and Braised Duck with Sauerkraut

TIME: 2 hours, largely unattended
MAKES: 4 servings

Here's a simple two-step procedure for duck, in which you first roast the bird, and then you braise it briefly. It keeps even the breast meat moist while making the legs ultra-tender. There are many options for the braising medium, but none provides more complementary flavor with less work than sauerkraut. The result is a moist bird with a sauce that doubles as a side vegetable. Although the cooking takes some time, you can practically ignore the duck as it roasts; if the oven temperature is moderate, it will brown more or less automatically and render its fat at the same time.

1 duck (about 4 pounds)
Salt and freshly ground black pepper
4 cups sauerkraut, rinsed
2 teaspoons sweet paprika
½ cup dry white wine or water
2 bay leaves

1 Preheat the oven to 375°F. Prick the duck all over with a fork, then sprinkle it with salt and pepper and place it in a large, deep, ovenproof skillet or Dutch oven. Roast the duck, checking occasionally to make sure it is browning steadily, for about 1½ hours. (If the duck is barely browning, increase the heat by 50 degrees; if it seems to be browning too quickly, reduce the heat slightly.) At that point, the duck will be nicely browned and have rendered a great deal of fat; pour off all but a few tablespoons of the fat and transfer the pan to the top of the stove. Don't worry if the duck does not appear to be fully cooked.

2 Scatter the sauerkraut around the duck, then sprinkle it with paprika, moisten it with the wine, and tuck the bay leaves in there. Turn the heat to low and cover. Simmer for about 15 minutes, then stir and put some of the sauerkraut on top of the duck.

3 Cook for another 15 minutes or so, until the duck is quite tender. Carve and serve.

WINE A dry Alsatian white, such as Pinot Blanc, Pinot Gris, or Riesling, or a Halbtrocken or Kabinett wine from Germany

SERVE WITH Rye bread and any root vegetable dish you like, or Steamed Broccoli (or Other Vegetable) (page 203)

SIMPLIFY THE PROCESS by roasting the bird in the same pan you plan to braise it in—a Dutch oven or a deep 12-inch skillet will handle the task perfectly.

THE BEST SAUERKRAUT is sold in bulk, but you can buy perfectly good sauerkraut in jars or plastic bags in the supermarket. Just make sure that the only ingredients are cabbage and salt (inferior sauerkraut contains preservatives, and that sold in cans tastes tinny).

| Unfortunately, a single duck provides skimpy servings for four people. You can make up for this with side dishes, but there are other solutions as well:

| Braise a piece of slab bacon and/or smoked or fresh pork along with the duck, after adding the sauerkraut; you'll have to increase the cooking time a bit.

| Peel and cut up some potatoes (or carrots, parsnips, or turnips) and cook them along with the duck and sauerkraut.

| Finally, you can simply cook more duck— start with two ducks, or add a couple of duck legs or, best of all, sear a duck breast—just brown it on both sides as you would a steak— and serve the slices separately.

Baked Eggs with Onions and Cheese

TIME: 30 to 40 minutes
MAKES: 4 servings

Baked eggs are little-known these days, but they are easy and underrated. I first encountered them combined with slow-cooked onions, cheese, and bread crumbs, a recipe taught me by a college friend whose family had been making it for years. The trick with baked eggs is to avoid overcooking, because the consistency of baked eggs should be like that of fried eggs, with a barely cooked white and a soft, runny yolk. This is a real joy here; when you cut into the yolk, it spills out over bread crumbs, melted cheese, and onions, moistening the lot. But just a minute too long in the oven and the yolk will become medium- or hard-cooked, and much of the pleasure will be lost.

4 tablespoons unsalted butter or olive oil

4 cups sliced onions

Salt and freshly ground black pepper

1½ cups coarse fresh bread crumbs

1 cup grated cheese, such as Gruyère or Emmentaler

½ cup grated Parmigiano-Reggiano cheese

8 extra-large eggs

1 Preheat the oven to 450°F. Put the butter or oil in a large, ovenproof skillet over medium-high heat. Add the onions and a liberal sprinkling of salt and pepper, cover the skillet, and turn the heat to medium. Cook, stirring occasionally, until the onions are very soft and tender but not browned, about 15 minutes.

2 Combine the bread crumbs and cheeses and sprinkle half this mixture over the onions. Use the back of a spoon to make eight little nests in the mixture and crack an egg into each. Top with some salt and pepper and the remaining bread-crumb-and-cheese mixture.

3 Bake for 5 minutes, or until the eggs are barely set; turn on the broiler and brown the top for a minute or so, but be careful not to overcook the eggs. Serve hot or at room temperature.

WINE Pinot Noir or Chardonnay

SERVE WITH Raw Beet Salad (page 194), Simple Green Salad (page 196), or simply carrot and celery sticks

THE EASIEST WAY to master the timing is to underbake the eggs slightly, then finish them under the broiler, keeping a careful eye on them all the while. Even then, overcooking is a danger, and it's better to remove them prematurely and let the heat of the pan finish the cooking, or return them to the broiler for another 30 seconds, than to allow the yolk to harden.

FRESH BREAD CRUMBS are best. To make them, just dry out a couple of slices of good bread in a low oven (or leave them out on the counter for a day or so), then grind coarsely in a food processor—coarse crumbs become crunchy rather than sandy when baked.

| Eggs can be baked on a bed of almost anything, from cooked spinach or sliced tomatoes to creamy polenta or mashed potatoes.

POT STICKERS

GRILLED FLANK STEAK WITH KIMCHEE-STYLE COLESLAW

BEEF WRAPPED IN LETTUCE LEAVES, KOREAN STYLE

SKIRT STEAK WITH COMPOUND BUTTER

SKIRT STEAK WITH PLUM PURÉE SAUCE

GRILLED STEAKS WITH ROQUEFORT SAUCE

STEAK WITH CHIMICHURRI SAUCE

RIB-EYE STEAKS WITH ANCHOVY-RED WINE SAUCE

ROAST SIRLOIN OF BEEF

ASIAN POT ROAST WITH TURNIPS

POT ROAST WITH CRANBERRIES

VEAL STEW

VIETNAMESE-STYLE PORK

SLOW-COOKED RIBS

PORK CUTLET WITH MISO-RED WINE SAUCE

FORTY-MINUTE CASSOULET

Meat

GRILLED LAMB RIBS

LAMB WITH PEACHES

LAMB WITH PEPPERS AND YOGURT SAUCE

BONELESS LAMB SHOULDER ROAST

GRILLED BONELESS LEG OF LAMB

Pot Stickers

TIME: 1 hour
MAKES: about 48 dumplings,
(4 main-course servings or
8 or more appetizer servings)

There is only one major hassle in making pot stickers, the fabulous, crisp-and-tender Chinese dumplings, and that is making the dough. But store-bought wrappers are now sold in just about every supermarket.

A filling of ground pork, cabbage, scallions, ginger and garlic can be put together in less than 10 minutes. Filling each wrapper takes about 30 seconds once you get the hang of it. This means that you can make four dozen dumplings in about half an hour. At that point they can be covered and refrigerated for several hours, or frozen for later use. Happily crammed in a skillet, they take less than 10 minutes. (You'll have to cook them in batches if you're making four dozen, but you can eat them in batches, too.) The dipping sauce adds 5 minutes.

¾ pound ground pork or other meat
1 cup finely minced cabbage
2 tablespoons minced ginger
1 tablespoon minced garlic
6 scallions, white and green parts separated, both finely minced
½ cup plus 2 tablespoons good soy sauce
48 dumpling wrappers (or a few more to allow for some failures), about 2 inches across
1 egg, lightly beaten
Peanut or vegetable oil
¼ cup rice or white vinegar

1 Combine the pork, cabbage, ginger, garlic, white parts of the scallions, and 2 tablespoons soy sauce in a bowl with ¼ cup water. Lay a wrapper on a clean, dry surface and, using your finger or a brush, spread a bit of egg along half of its circumference. Place a rounded teaspoon or so of the filling in the center of the wrapper, fold over, and seal by pinching the edges together. Lay each dumpling on a plate until you're ready to cook. If you want to wait a few hours, keep the plate covered with plastic wrap and refrigerate until mealtime, or freeze for few days.

2 To cook, pour about 2 tablespoons oil into a large non-stick skillet, turn the heat to medium-high and heat for a minute. Add the dumplings, one at a time, to the oil; you can crowd them to the point where they touch one another, but they should still sit flat in one layer. Cook for about 2 minutes, or until the bottoms of the dumplings are lightly browned. Add ¼ cup water per dozen dumplings to the skillet (in other words, if you're

WINE Dry Pinot Blanc, Tokay, or Riesling from Alsace, or beer
SERVE WITH These are traditionally served as an appetizer before a meal, but served with stir-fried vegetables, they make a full meal.

cooking 2 dozen dumplings at a time, add ½ cup water) and cover; lower the heat to medium and cook for 3 minutes. Meanwhile, to make the dipping sauce, combine the remaining ½ cup soy sauce with the green parts of the scallions and vinegar and stir.

3 After about 3 minutes, uncover the dumplings, raise the heat again, and cook for another 1 to 2 minutes, until the bottoms are dark brown and crisp and the water is evaporated. (Use another 2 tablespoons oil to repeat the process, if necessary.) Serve hot, with the dipping sauce.

Keys To SUCCESS

ALWAYS USE the round wrappers, as the square kind result in too much empty dough.

IT HELPS to incorporate a little water into the filling, which, combined with the meat juices, keeps the interior super-moist.

FOLDING THE dumplings is almost intuitive; you will quickly get into it. To seal, you brush an edge of the dough with a little beaten egg. (Water will work as a "glue" also, but not quite as well, and you only need 1 egg for a whole batch of dumplings, so it's worth it.)

THE COOKING technique is unusual but simple: Brown the dumplings for a couple of minutes in oil, then add a little water, cover for 3 or 4 minutes, then uncover and finish the browning. It works.

With MINIMAL Effort

Vegetarian Pot Stickers: Make the filling using 2 cups finely minced cabbage, 1 cup minced shiitakes (caps only), ½ cup minced scallions or chives, and the ginger, garlic, and soy as above (omit the water). Proceed precisely as above.

Shrimp Pot Stickers: Make the filling using 2 cups peeled and finely minced shrimp (start with about 1 pound unpeeled shrimp), ½ cup trimmed and minced snow peas, ½ cup minced shallots, and the ginger, garlic, and soy as above. Add 1 tablespoon toasted sesame oil (or 1 tablespoon minced bacon) to the mix, then proceed as above.

| The fillings can be almost anything: Ground pork or beef, chicken, turkey, or even lamb will produce the most familiar kind of pot sticker. These can be all meat or, like the ones above, meat mixed with cabbage (meat mixed with chopped shiitake mushrooms is good, too). Cabbage can dominate in a vegetarian dumpling, as above, or you can use a variety of vegetables and herbs—chives or scallions are especially great in large quantity.

Grilled Flank Steak with Kimchee-Style Coleslaw

TIME: 1 hour or more, largely unattended
MAKES: 4 servings

Most kimchee, Korea's famous cabbage pickle, takes a while to make. But it's easy enough to take the basic ingredients and flavors of kimchee and create a fast cabbage salad that puts ordinary coleslaw to shame. Use this as a flavorful bed for simply grilled beef, or anything else that has the flavor to stand up to the spicy slaw, and you have a great summer dish. Cook the meat in a skillet or under the broiler if the weather is cold.

1 small head Napa or Savoy cabbage (about 1½ pounds)

Coarse salt

3 spring onions or 6 large scallions, trimmed and chopped

3 garlic cloves or to taste, minced

1 tablespoon *co chu karo* chile powder (see Keys to Success) or crushed red pepper flakes, or to taste

1 tablespoon minced ginger

3 tablespoons fish sauce or soy sauce

2 tablespoons rice wine or other vinegar

About 1½ pounds flank steak

Freshly ground black pepper

1 Remove the tough exterior leaves of the cabbage and core it by cutting a cone-shaped wedge out of the stem end. Shred it by cutting thin slices and separating them with your hands. Put in a colander and toss with about 1 tablespoon salt and the onions. Let sit for at least 1 hour, preferably 2, tossing occasionally, until the cabbage wilts.

2 Meanwhile, start a medium-hot charcoal or wood fire or preheat a gas grill to the maximum. Set the rack 2-4 inches from the heat source. For the dressing, combine the garlic, chile powder, ginger, fish sauce, and vinegar in a bowl. Grill the steak for about 4 minutes per side for medium-rare, turning once, longer or shorter according to the degree of doneness you prefer. Sprinkle the steak with salt and pepper as it cooks.

3 Remove the steak from the grill and let it rest while you squeeze as much liquid as you can out of the cabbage and toss it with the dressing. To serve, carve the steak. Place a portion of cabbage on a plate and top with a few slices of steak. Spoon a little of the dressing over the steak and serve.

WINE Beer

SERVE WITH Easy Rice (page 204), or Rice Salad with Peas and Soy (page 200)

QUICK KIMCHEE takes very little work, but the cabbage itself is best if salted and allowed to sit for an hour or even longer. This process draws out excess water and makes the cabbage ultra-crisp. You can skip the step if you're pressed for time; the salad will taste just as good.

KIMCHEE OF any type packs a potent punch, thanks to prodigious amounts of garlic and chile peppers. I've included "appropriate" quantities of those here, and you can even increase the amounts if you like— though many people will find these proportions quite strong enough.

IF YOU CAN get to a Korean market, buy some of the ground chile powder labeled *co chu karo*, which is hot but also quite flavorful. Otherwise substitute any good ground chiles or the standard crushed red pepper flakes. Fish sauce is traditional (dried oysters or dried shrimp are even more traditional, but fish sauce has the same character); you can use soy sauce if you prefer.

| Add some shredded vegetables to the cabbage: red bell peppers, carrots, daikon radish, and/or jicama, for example.

| Substitute grilled pork, shrimp, tuna, or chicken (legs, for best flavor) for the beef.

Beef Wrapped in Lettuce Leaves, Korean Style

TIME: 45 minutes, longer if you have the time

MAKES: 4 servings

For *bulgogi,* a Korean beef dish sometimes made with short ribs, the meat is stripped off the bone, marinated in a soy-based sauce, and then grilled at the table; the hot meat is then wrapped in cool lettuce and eaten with the hands. I had thought the dish was impossible to attempt without an in-table-grill. I finally realized, however, that the time the meat spends over the coals—certainly less than 5 minutes—might be long enough to add the mental image of wood flavor, but certainly not the reality. So, with what might be described as typical American arrogance, I set about reinventing this traditional Korean dish, and I'm happy about the results.

3 to 4 pounds short ribs

½ cup roughly chopped trimmed scallions, shallots, or onion

1 tablespoon roughly chopped ginger

6 garlic cloves, roughly chopped

1 tablespoon sugar

½ teaspoon freshly ground black pepper

½ cup soy sauce

16 to 24 romaine or other lettuce leaves, washed and dried

Soy sauce or ground bean paste (available at Asian markets), optional

1 If time allows, freeze the meat for 30 minutes or so to facilitate slicing. Use a sharp knife to strip the meat from the ribs—it will come off easily and in one piece (reserve the bones and any meat that adheres to them for stock).

2 Combine the scallions, ginger, garlic, sugar, pepper, soy sauce, and ½ cup water in a blender and purée until very smooth. Slice the meat into pieces between ⅛ and ¼ inch in thickness. Toss with the marinade and let sit from 15 minutes to 2 hours. Preheat a grill, broiler with the grill rack set 2 to 4 inches from the heat source. Or preheat a stovetop grill, or preheat the oven to its maximum heat and put a heavy roasting pan in it (see Keys to Success).

3 Remove the meat from the marinade and grill, pan-grill, broil, or roast it, just until done, no more than a couple of minutes per side; it's nice if the meat is browned on the outside and rare on the inside, but it's imperative

WINE Beer or green tea

SERVE WITH If you live near a Korean store, buy a variety of Korean kimchee and pickles and serve them along with Kimchee-Style Coleslaw (page 152). Nearly-Instant Miso Soup with Tofu (page 4), is a good starter.

that it not be overcooked. Serve with the lettuce leaves. To eat, wrap a piece or two of meat in a torn piece of lettuce; garnish with a drop or two of soy sauce or bean paste, if you like.

Pork, Mushrooms, or Chicken Wrapped in Lettuce Leaves, Korean Style: For the beef, substitute grilled strips of pork, shiitake or portobello mushrooms, or boneless chicken.

This meat is also good served on rice.

Keys To SUCCESS

FREEZING THE meat slightly before stripping it from the bones makes the process easier, but it's not essential.

GRILLING REMAINS the best cooking technique—a couple of minutes over a very hot fire is ideal—but a stovetop grill or very hot skillet works nearly as well, as long as you have a powerful exhaust fan to suck out the smoke. Alternatively, a good broiler will do the trick; just turn the slices once. Finally, if you set an iron skillet or heavy roasting pan in an oven heated to its maximum, then throw the meat onto that, it will sear the meat and cook it through in a couple of minutes.

NO MATTER how you cook the meat, do not sacrifice internal juices for external browning; that is, it's better to serve lightly browned but moist meat than tough, overcooked meat with a lovely crust.

Skirt Steak with Compound Butter

We have my friend Steve Johnson (chef at the Blue Room in Cambridge, Massachusetts) to thank for this particular combination of skirt steak and compound butter. But you can hardly go wrong with skirt steak, a long, thin band of wonderfully marbled muscle (actually the cow's diaphragm), or with the flavored butter that complements it. Until butter became forbidden food it was a common treatment as a quick flavor booster, even plain. In classic cooking, compound butters were kept on hand and often used to enhance rich sauces. But more recently they've stood on their own, as quick, simple toppings, not only for steak, but for leaner meats, like veal, chicken, and even fish.

Skirt Steak with Shallot-Thyme Butter

½ cup (1 stick) unsalted butter, softened slightly

¼ teaspoon fresh thyme leaves

10 chives, minced

1 shallot, minced

Salt and freshly ground black pepper

½ teaspoon red wine vinegar or fresh lemon juice

About 24 ounces skirt steak, cut into 4 portions

1 Prepare a gas or charcoal grill: The fire should be so hot, you can hold your hand over it for only a couple of seconds. (You can broil or pan-grill the steak, if you prefer.) Meanwhile, cream the butter with a fork, then add and integrate the thyme, chives, shallot, about ½ teaspoon each of salt and pepper, and the vinegar. Taste and add more of any ingredient you deem necessary.

2 When the fire is ready, grill the steak, 2 minutes per side for rare, 1 to 2 minutes longer for medium-rare to medium. Season the steak as it cooks with salt and pepper.

3 Spread each steak with about a tablespoon of the flavored butter and serve. Wrap and refrigerate or freeze the remaining butter for future use.

WINE Rhône varietals, Cabernet, inexpensive Bordeaux, or Zinfandel—any wine that is not too subtle

SERVE WITH Easy Rice (page 204), and/or Steamed Broccoli (or Other Vegetable) (page 203), topped with a little of the butter; Sautéed Shiitake Mushrooms, (page 202); Roasted Peppers (page 195); Simple Green Salad (page 196)

GOOD BUTTER is an essential starting place, but this need not mean the 8-dollar-a-pound kind from Normandy (although that certainly won't hurt). Generally, unsalted butter is of higher quality than the salted kind, and any good brand, as long as it is fresh, will do fine.

THE EASIEST way to make compound butter is to mince all the flavorings and then cream them and the butter together with a fork, just as you would butter and sugar in making a cake. But if your butter is ice cold (or frozen), use a small food processor to combine all the ingredients quickly; there will be some waste, as you'll never get all the butter out of the container and blade, but the process will take just seconds.

SKIRT STEAK, which was not easy to get even a couple of years ago, is now almost ubiquitous. It costs as much as 10 dollars a pound, but can often be found for well under half that, especially in supermarkets. It's a moist, juicy steak, but not exactly tender—a little chewier than good strip steak—and does not respond well to overcooking. If someone insists on having it cooked beyond medium-rare, take no responsibility.

All of these proportions are based on ½ cup (1 stick) butter. Remember that all of the flavoring can be done to taste; start with the suggested amounts and take it from there:

Horseradish (or Wasabi) and Ginger Butter with Soy: Flavor the butter with 1 teaspoon prepared horseradish or wasabi, 1 teaspoon finely minced ginger, and 1 teaspoon good soy sauce. Use salt and pepper sparingly.

Garlic-Oregano Butter: Flavor the butter with 1 teaspoon finely minced garlic (or 1 tablespoon roasted garlic puree), 1 teaspoon finely minced fresh oregano or marjoram, and 1 teaspoon fresh lemon juice, along with salt and plenty of freshly ground black pepper.

Chile-Cilantro Butter: Flavor the butter with 1 stemmed, seeded, and finely minced small chile, 1 tablespoon minced cilantro, and 1 teaspoon fresh lime juice, along with salt and freshly ground black pepper.

Once you get started you'll see that compound butters can be made with any seasoning you like: mustard, garlic, ginger, chiles, vinegar, or citrus juice and zest, just to name a few. In summer and fall, you can easily experiment with adding the fresh herb of your choice—chervil is especially nice, as are dill and parsley.

Skirt Steak with Plum Purée Sauce

TIME: 40 to 50 minutes
MAKES: 4 servings

Most summer fruits are more capable of making a contribution to the savory part of a meal than we realize, especially when they're puréed, creating an easy-to-make base for an unusual sauce. This is a good example, an enriched, slightly sour purée of fresh plums that complements steak brilliantly.

3 tablespoons butter

1 cup plum purée (see Keys to Success)

Salt and freshly ground black pepper

About 24 ounces skirt steak, cut into 4 portions

⅛ teaspoon cayenne, or to taste

1 tablespoon fresh lemon juice

2 tablespoons minced fresh parsley

1 Prepare a gas or charcoal grill; the fire should be so hot you can hold your hand over it for only a couple of seconds. (You can broil or pan-grill the steak if you prefer.) Meanwhile, place the butter in a small saucepan and turn the heat to medium. Cook, shaking the pan occasionally, until the butter turns light brown, about 5 minutes. Lower the heat and stir in the purée. Cook, stirring, for about a minute; keep warm.

2 When the fire is ready, grill the steak, 2 minutes per side for rare, 1 to 2 minutes longer for medium-rare to medium. Season the steak as it cooks with salt and pepper.

3 While the steak is cooking, add the cayenne, lemon juice, and a pinch of salt to the purée and stir; taste and adjust the seasoning if necessary. Serve the steak with the sauce, garnished with the parsley.

WINE Rioja or another soft, lush red
SERVE WITH Roasted Peppers (page 195), and/or Tomato Salad with Basil (page 198); Sautéed Shiitake Mushrooms (page 202)

THE PLUMS must be ripe, even a tad overripe, making this an ideal dish for using up fruit you might otherwise discard.

TO PEEL, plunge the plums into boiling water for about 30 seconds, or until the skin loosens (sometimes this takes as long as a minute); then plunge them into ice water to stop the cooking. At that point, you can easily remove the skins with a paring knife. Then cut the fruit into halves or quarters and remove the pits. Generally, figure that about a pound of fruit will produce just over a cup purée.

TO PURÉE, cram the plums into the blender, literally pushing them down onto the blades and squeezing some of the water from them. This will help get the machine started and should make it easy to purée the fruit without any intervention or added liquid. If the machine is having trouble, turn it off and use a wooden spoon or rubber spatula to mash the fruit down onto the blades.

THE PURÉE is stable, but its flavor is fleeting and will become less intense with every passing hour. If you are not ready to proceed after making it, refrigerate in a tightly covered container and use within a day.

Skirt Steak with Peach or Apricot Purée Sauce: Make the purée using peaches or apricots; these will take a little more lemon juice and cayenne.

| For the skirt steak, substitute sirloin strip or rib eye, pork chops or ribs, or lamb steaks.

Grilled Steaks with Roquefort Sauce

TIME: 30 to 40 minutes

MAKES: 4 servings

It may be that the paradigm of steak-and-cheese combinations is the Philly cheese steak, but there is a more elegant and arguably better-tasting way to combine these two foods: Top steak with a simple sauce based on blue cheese. This dish, which often appears on bistro menus in France, fits the need for a good steak served with something powerfully salty and rich (anchovy butter, or a combination of butter, soy sauce, and ginger also does the trick). Some might consider the sauce overkill, but not those of us who crave it.

1 tablespoon butter or grape-seed, corn, or other light oil

¼ cup minced shallots

2 tablespoons white wine vinegar or cider vinegar

6 ounces Roquefort or other blue cheese, crumbled

Generous pinch of cayenne

Salt

1½ to 2 pounds strip steaks, filet mignon, or rib-eye steaks

Minced fresh parsley or chives, optional

1 Start a hot charcoal or wood fire, preheat a gas grill to the maximum, or preheat the broiler. The fire should be quite hot, and the grill rack no more than 4 inches from the heat source.

2 Put the butter in a small saucepan and turn the heat to medium. When the butter melts and its foam begins to subside, add the shallots and cook until soft, stirring occasionally, about 5 minutes. Add the vinegar, stir, and cook until it is just about evaporated, 1 to 2 minutes. Turn the heat to low and stir in the cheese and cayenne. Stir occasionally until the cheese melts, then taste and adjust the seasoning as necessary (it's unlikely that the sauce will need any salt). Keep warm while you grill the steaks.

3 Season the steaks well with salt, then grill or broil for 3 to 4 minutes per side for medium-rare, or longer or shorter according to your taste. Serve the steaks with a spoonful or two of sauce ladled over each, garnished with the parsley, if you like.

WINE Rioja, Dolcetto, or another red from Spain or Northern Italy

SERVE WITH Simple Green Salad (page 196) or Tomato Salad with Basil (page 198); Mashed Potatoes (page 205), or Crisp Potatoes (page 206); Steamed Broccoli (or Other Vegetable) (page 203)

ROQUEFORT, which is made from sheep's milk, is my favorite blue for this sauce. But it's entirely a matter of taste—Stilton, Gorgonzola, Maytag blue, or any high-quality, fairly soft blue cheese will work equally well. Don't bother, however, trying to make this sauce with commercially produced domestic blue cheese, such as that sold precrumbled for salads. Not only will its taste be inferior, but it will not give the sauce the same creaminess.

THIS IS an instance in which the usually too-lean and mildly flavored tenderloin (filet mignon) will do just fine. Its tenderness is welcome, and its blandness is more than compensated for by the sauce. I'd still prefer a good strip steak or rib eye, which are chewier and more flavorful, but you will notice their higher fat content when they're combined with the rich sauce.

| This is equally good with pan-grilled pork chops or thick medallions of pork tenderloin (buy a piece of tenderloin and cut it cross-wise into ¾-inch thick slices), or thin cutlets of veal or pork, sauteed.

Steak with Chimichurri Sauce

This simple, Argentine steak sauce is made almost entirely from parsley, with relatively huge amounts of chopped garlic and red pepper. In spirit, it's not unlike pesto, but because everything is hand-chopped rather than ground or mashed, it has a bit more chew to it. And its powerful ingredients set it apart, making it the perfect complement for mild-tasting but meaty tenderloin.

¾ cup washed, dried, and chopped fresh parsley (about 1 large bunch)

½ cup extra virgin olive oil

¼ cup fresh lemon juice

2 tablespoons finely chopped garlic

2 teaspoons crushed red pepper flakes

Salt and freshly ground black pepper

24 ounces beef tenderloin steaks, each about 1 inch thick

1 Put the parsley in a bowl and whisk in the oil, along with the lemon juice, garlic, crushed red pepper, and salt. Taste and adjust the seasoning if necessary; let the sauce rest at room temperature for an hour or two if you have time.

2 Put a large skillet over high heat and heat for 1 to 2 minutes. Meanwhile, season the steaks with salt and pepper. When the skillet is hot, add the steaks and cook for about 3 minutes per side for medium-rare, or a little longer for medium. Leave the steaks whole or slice them; serve with the chimichurri spooned over them, passing more sauce at the table.

WINE Inexpensive, rough red, like a no-name Cabernet or Zinfandel

SERVE WITH Simple Green Salad (page 196), Rice Salad with Peas and Soy (page 200), or Cornbread (page 209)

YOU ALMOST cannot use too much garlic or red pepper here; cut back on the amounts if you like, but chimichurri should be powerful.

THE SAUCE can be made several hours ahead (in fact it's better that way); keep it at room temperature. If you're going to keep it longer than that—up to a day or so—refrigerate, then bring it back to room temperature before serving.

| Use the sauce on grilled pork or lamb chops; grilled or roasted leg of lamb; or grilled, broiled, or roasted chicken thighs.

Rib-Eye Steaks with Anchovy-Red Wine Sauce

TIME: 30 to 40 minutes
MAKES: 4 servings

Another great, simple sauce based on anchovies (there are two in the pasta chapter; see pages 30 and 40). You get acidity, astringency, and fruitiness from the wine, piquancy from the garlic and anchovy, complexity from the thyme, and a smooth finish from the butter—all in about the time it takes to prepare a grill for the steaks.

2 cups fruity but sturdy red wine, such as Côtes du Rhone, Zinfandel, or California Cabernet

½ teaspoon minced garlic

6 anchovy fillets, with some of their oil

1 teaspoon fresh thyme leaves

2 tablespoons unsalted butter

Salt and freshly ground black pepper

4 rib-eye steaks, each about 6 ounces (or 2 larger steaks)

1 Pour the wine into a small saucepan and turn the heat to high. Reduce, stirring occasionally, to about ½ cup. Meanwhile, start a hot charcoal or wood fire or preheat a gas grill to the maximum with the grill rack set 2 to 4 inches above the heat source.

2 When the wine is reduced, lower the heat so the reduction simmers and stir in the garlic, anchovies, and thyme. Cook, stirring occasionally, until the anchovies dissolve. When the grill is ready, cook the steaks for about 3 minutes per side for medium rare, or a little longer or shorter according to your preference.

3 Beat the butter into the sauce until it is smooth, then season to taste. Slice the steaks, drizzle with the sauce, and serve.

WINE The same as, or similar to, the wine you use in the sauce

SERVE WITH 60-Minute Bread (page 207) or good store-bought bread; Tomato Salad with Basil (page 198) or Simple Green Salad (page 196); Mashed Potatoes (page 205) or Crisp Potatoes (page 206); Sautéed Shiitake Mushrooms (page 202)

FOR MORE INFORMATION about anchovies, see page 31.

YOU DON'T NEED great red wine for this sauce, but it should be one with a fair amount of fruit and at least a little structure—which rules out inexpensive Merlot or Pinot Noir.

| Sauté the garlic and anchovies in a couple of tablespoons of olive oil (and anchovy oil) before adding to the wine for a somewhat more subtle flavor.

| Garnish the steaks with chopped parsley, basil, or a few thyme leaves.

| Substitute ¼ cup chopped shallots for the garlic.

Roast Sirloin of Beef

Few meats are as tender, juicy, and flavorful as roast beef, yet none is easier to prepare, given the appropriate cut and proper technique. Two of the best cuts for roasting, filet (or tenderloin) and standing rib are not always ideal. The first is supremely tender, but expensive and nearly tasteless; the second tends to be sold in large cuts that are too unwieldy for most weeknights. But the sirloin strip, also called New York strip—the same cut that makes for some of the best steaks— cut in a single large piece, is perfect. Ask your butcher for a 2- or 3-pound piece of sirloin strip—essentially a steak cut as a roast—and you should have it within minutes.

One 2½- to 3-pound piece sirloin strip

Salt and freshly ground black pepper

1 Preheat the oven to 500°F with a skillet large enough to hold the roast in the oven so it preheats as well. Sprinkle the meat liberally with salt and pepper.

2 When the oven and pan are hot, add the roast to the pan, top (fatty) side down and roast for 10 minutes. Turn and roast fatty side up for 10 more minutes. Turn and roast for 5 minutes, then turn again and roast for 5 minutes. Total cooking time is 30 minutes.

3 At this point the roast will be nicely browned all over. When a meat thermometer inserted into the center of the meat, about 1 inch from one of the ends, registers 120°F, the meat will be rare to medium-rare. Cook longer if you like, but beware that from this point on it will increase a stage of doneness every 3 to 5 minutes.

4 Let the roast rest for 5 to 10 minutes, then carve and serve, with its juices.

WINE Good Bordeaux or Burgundy, or decent Rioja
SERVE WITH 60-Minute Bread (page 207) or good store-bought bread; Tomato Salad with Basil (page 198); or Simple Green Salad (page 196); Mashed Potatoes (page 205) or Crisp Potatoes (page 206); Sautéed Shiitake Mushrooms (page 202) or Steamed Broccoli (or Other Vegetable) (page 203)

SOME BUTCHERS may insist on tucking the "tail" of the meat under the larger section and tying the whole thing as a roast, and although you can let them, it's far from essential.

A MEAT thermometer can help you judge doneness, and it pays to undercook the meat slightly and let it sit for a few minutes before carving; this not only makes carving easier, but it also prevents overcooking.

YOU CAN serve thick, steaklike slices, or carve the meat more thinly, as you would a traditional roast beef. Either way, you can serve the slices as they are, or make a quick sauce for them (see With Minimal Effort).

IT'S WORTH noting that this technique will work for larger roasts of sirloin as well, and because the meat is of more-or-less uniform thickness, cooking time will not be appreciably longer for a roast of 4 or 5 pounds than it is for one of 2 or 3 pounds.

Roast Beef with Gravy: To make pan gravy, discard all but 1 to 2 tablespoons of the fat remaining in the pan. Put the pan over high heat and add 1 cup red wine, chicken or beef stock, or water and cook, stirring frequently, until the mixture is reduced to about ½ cup. Stir in a tablespoon or more of butter, a few drops of lemon juice, and salt and pepper to taste. Serve with the beef.

Roast Beef with Red Wine Sauce: Combine 2 cups red wine with ¼ cup minced shallots or 1 tablespoon slivered garlic and reduce over high heat until only about ½ cup of syrupy liquid remains. Stir in a tablespoon of butter and some salt and pepper. Serve with the beef.

Asian Pot Roast with Turnips

TIME: 3 to 4 hours, largely unattended
MAKES: 4 servings

Pot roast is a true no-brainer—since it is always cooked well-done, timing is pretty flexible, and since it is cooked in a covered pot with liquid, neither source nor level of heat matters much. You can cook it on top of the stove or in the oven, at a very low heat, something more moderate, or even quite high. You can even cook it in advance and reheat it, or cut the meat up before cooking and call it beef stew.

The best part is that flavoring pot roast is no more than a matter of taste; you can hardly go wrong. And when you combine Asian seasonings with this classic European technique, the results are unusually wonderful.

1 tablespoon peanut or vegetable oil

3- to 4-pound brisket or boneless chuck

⅓ cup dark soy sauce, or ½ cup light soy sauce

5 nickel-sized slices of ginger (don't bother to peel)

4 pieces star anise

2 to 3 cups peeled and cubed white turnips or rutabaga

½ cup trimmed and minced scallions

1 Pour the oil into a large skillet, turn the heat to high, and heat for a minute. Add the roast (you can cover the pot loosely to reduce spattering) and sear for about 5 minutes on each side, or until nicely browned. While the meat is browning, combine the soy sauce, ginger, anise, and 2 cups of water in a casserole just big enough to hold the meat snugly. Bring this mixture to a boil, then adjust the heat so that it simmers.

2 When the meat is browned, add it to the simmering liquid and cover the pot. Cook over medium-low heat, turning the meat once or twice an hour and adding more water if necessary, for about 3 hours, or until the meat is just about tender (poke it with a thin-bladed knife; when the meat is done, the knife will meet little resistance). Fish out and discard the star anise and add the turnips, stirring to make sure it is coated with liquid (again, add more water if necessary). Replace the cover and cook until the turnips are very tender, about 30 minutes.

WINE Syrah or a sturdy Cabernet Sauvignon

SERVE WITH Easy Rice (page 204) (or, for the European version, buttered noodles) or Crisp Pan-Fried Noodle Cake (page 212); Steamed Broccoli (or Other Vegetable) (page 203)

3 Remove the meat and carve it, then return it to the pot (or place it on a platter with the sauce and the turnips). Garnish with the scallions and serve.

Keys To SUCCESS

TENDER CUTS of beef, like sirloin and even tenderloin, will markedly reduce the cooking time, but will not produce the same rich, silky sauce created by the tougher cuts. Thus inexpensive cuts like chuck or brisket are best—and you can use either one. Chuck becomes tender a little faster, but it is fattier; brisket becomes a little more dry, but the sauce takes care of that, and it slices beautifully.

YOU CAN SKIP browning the meat to save time (and mess) if necessary. Yes, browning creates complexity, but there is so much flavor in this dish you won't miss it.

MAKE SURE the liquid in the pot doesn't evaporate. This is the best reason to keep the heat fairly low, as high heat will quickly boil out the liquid. Add liquid if necessary.

WHEN YOU'RE making a pot roast, the vegetables you add at the beginning contribute to the development of the sauce, but those at the end draw on the sauce for flavor, often making them the best part.

With MINIMAL Effort

European Pot Roast with Carrots: Use olive oil for searing. Omit the soy, water, ginger, and anise mixture, using instead a mixture of 2 cups red wine, 20 peeled pearl onions (the frozen ones aren't bad), 5 lightly smashed garlic cloves, and 1 cup trimmed and chopped mushrooms. Add more wine (or water) if necessary to the simmering meat as it cooks. Substitute carrots for the turnips in step 3 and garnish with chopped parsley in place of the scallions.

Pot Roast with Cranberries

Unlike their cousin, the blueberry—which is sometimes used in savory cooking, although almost never successfully—cranberries are not at all sweet, and so make a much more natural companion for meat. This is a gutsy, appealing, and unusual pot roast, and one you can make quickly or slowly, depending on your time, taste, and budget.

1 tablespoon butter or extra virgin olive oil

½ cup sugar

2- to 3-pound piece of chuck or brisket

Salt and freshly ground black pepper

½ cup sherry vinegar or good wine vinegar

12 ounces fresh or frozen cranberries

1 orange

Cayenne

1 Put the butter in a casserole or skillet and turn the heat to medium-high. Put the sugar on a plate and dredge the meat in it until all the surfaces are coated. Reserve the remaining sugar. When the butter foam subsides, brown the meat on all sides—this will take about 15 minutes—seasoning it with salt and pepper as it browns.

2 When the meat is nicely browned, add the vinegar and cook for a minute, stirring. Add the cranberries and remaining sugar and stir. Strip the zest from the orange (you can do it in broad strips, with a small knife or vegetable peeler) and add it to the skillet. Juice the orange and add the juice also, along with a pinch of cayenne. Turn the heat to low and cover; the mixture should bubble but not furiously.

3 Cook, turning the meat and stirring about every 30 minutes, for 2 hours or longer, or until the meat is tender. When the meat is done, taste and adjust the seasoning if necessary. Turn off the heat and let the roast rest for a few minutes, then carve and serve, with the sauce.

WINE Rioja, Merlot, or another soft red

SERVE WITH 60-Minute Bread (page 207) or good store-bought bread; Steamed Broccoli (or Other Vegetable) (page 203) or Glazed Carrots (page 201); Mashed Potatoes (page 205) or Crisp Potatoes (page 206)

DUSTING THE MEAT with some of the sugar makes the browning process go much more rapidly, and leaves behind a caramelized residue that is deglazed by the vinegar when you add it. All of this lends complexity to the final dish.

MOST POT ROASTS depend for their flavor on the juices exuded by the meat itself; that's why tough, slow-cooking cuts like brisket or chuck are usually preferable. But since the meat's contribution here is minimized by the powerful cranberry-based combination, a faster-cooking cut like tenderloin works perfectly, reducing the cooking time to just over an hour (see With Minimal Effort).

Faster Pot Roast with Cranberries: Substitute a 2-to 3-pound piece of tenderloin (filet mignon) for the chuck or brisket and reduce the cooking time to about 1 hour, or until the internal temperature is 125° to 130°F (medium-rare); you can cook it longer than that if you like.

Veal Stew

Veal Stew of Spring

The charm of most braised dishes is that they result in succulent, tender meat, and require little attention after an initial browning. The sad truth, however, is that most meats need hours—sometimes many hours—before they become truly tender. Not so with veal chunks taken from the shoulder or leg, which become tender in less than an hour and produce a superb stew.

1 tablespoon extra virgin olive oil

1 tablespoon butter (or use more oil)

1½ to 2 pounds veal chunks, cut into pieces no larger than 1½ inches in any dimension

1 sprig fresh tarragon, or ½ teaspoon dried tarragon

1 pound spring onions, shallots, or scallions, peeled or trimmed and cut in half if large

Salt and freshly ground black pepper

½ cup white wine or water

1 cup fresh shelled peas, snow peas, or frozen peas

1 Put a 12-inch skillet over high heat and heat for a minute. Add the oil and butter. When the butter melts, add the meat in one layer (if you use the larger amount of meat you may have to cook it in batches in order to cook only in one layer; it's worth the effort). Cook, undisturbed, until the meat is nicely browned on the bottom, about 5 minutes.

2 Add the tarragon, onions, and salt and pepper. Cook, stirring occasionally, until the onions soften and any bits of meat stuck to the bottom of the pan are released, about 5 minutes. Add the wine, stir, reduce the heat to low, and cover. Cook for 30 to 40 minutes, or until the veal is tender.

3 Uncover, add the peas, and raise the heat to medium. Cook for about 5 minutes more, until the peas are done. Taste and adjust the seasoning if necessary, and serve.

WINE Chardonnay, a light Zinfandel, or Pinot Noir

SERVE WITH 60-Minute Bread (page 207) or good store-bought bread; buttered noodles, Easy Rice (page 204), Mashed Potatoes (page 205), or Crisp Potatoes (page 206); Sautéed Shiitake Mushrooms (page 202); Simple Green Salad (page 196)

THE SMALLER the chunks of meat the quicker the cooking time. (This is a very basic and oft-ignored general principle of cooking: Spend a little more time with the knife and you sometimes spend a lot less time at the stove.) Smaller chunks have another advantage as well: In just a few minutes, enough of their surface area browns so that you can move to the next step of the recipe. This guarantees a full-flavored stew.

WHEN YOU are browning the meat, keep the heat high and do not move it around. Check one piece and, only when it appears good and browned underneath, proceed to the next step; it's really only necessary to brown one side.

DON'T ADD too much liquid; the meat and onions generate plenty of their own as the covered meat simmers gently.

Veal Stew, Provençal Style: In step 1, use all olive oil. In step 2, omit the tarragon and onions, adding instead 2 crushed garlic cloves, 20 roughly chopped basil leaves, 2 cups seeded and chopped tomatoes (canned are fine; drain them lightly), and 1 cup good black olives. Omit the wine or water. Add the salt and pepper and cook as above. In step 3, omit the peas; uncover and reduce the liquid if necessary until the stew is thick. Garnish with more chopped basil.

Veal Stew with Bacon and Mushrooms: In step 1, render ¼ pound chopped slab bacon in 1 tablespoon olive oil until crisp. Remove with a slotted spoon, then brown the veal in the bacon fat (pour some off first if it seems excessive). In step 2, omit the tarragon; cook the onions with a few sprigs of thyme (or 1 teaspoon dried thyme) and 1 cup trimmed and chopped mushrooms. After the onions soften, add the liquid as above. In step 3, return the bacon to the pan (you can add the peas or not, as you like) and cook for about 5 minutes more. Garnish and serve.

Veal Stew with Paprika: In step 1, use all butter (or grapeseed, corn, or other light oil). In step 2, omit the tarragon; add 2 crushed garlic cloves, and 2 teaspoons good paprika. Add salt, pepper, and liquid and cook as above. In step 3, omit the peas and stir in 1 cup sour cream and more paprika, if necessary.

Vietnamese-Style Pork

This dish has the beguiling, distinctively‍ Southeast Asian aroma of garlic—lots of it—nuoc mam (the Vietnamese fish sauce known more commonly by its Thai name, nam pla), and lime. But there are a couple of "secret" ingredients as well, including mildly acidic lemongrass and spicy black pepper in large quantities. Traditionally, this dish also contains caramelized sugar, which contributes a burnt sweetness but the intense heat of the grill makes honey a good substitute, and a much easier one. So the marinade can be assembled in 10 minutes, the grill preheated in another 10, and the pork grilled in 10: a great, intensely flavored, 30-minute dish.

2 tablespoons minced lemongrass

1 tablespoon minced garlic

3 tablespoons honey

1 tablespoon nam pla (Thai fish sauce), or to taste (you may substitute soy sauce)

2 limes

Freshly ground black pepper

1½ pounds country-style pork chops, preferably boneless

Chopped Thai basil, mint, cilantro, or a combination, optional

1 Combine the lemongrass, garlic, honey, and nam pla in a bowl; whisk to blend. Add the juice of 1 lime and lots of pepper—about a teaspoon. Marinate the pork in this mixture while you start a charcoal or wood fire, preheat a gas grill to the maximum, or preheat a broiler; the fire should be moderately hot, and the grill rack should be about 4 inches from the heat source.

2 Grill or broil the pork, spooning the marinade over it as it cooks, until done, about 10 minutes. Turn only once, so that each side browns nicely. Serve with wedges of lime, garnished with the optional herb.

WINE Beer, Champagne, or light Gewürztraminer
SERVE WITH Crisp Pan-fried Noodle Cake (page 212), Cold Noodles with Sesame (or Peanut) Sauce (page 210), Rice Salad with Peas and Soy (page 200); Green Salad with Soy Vinaigrette (page 197)

YOU CAN use pork chops for this dish, but so-called country-style ribs (actually the shoulder end of the pork loin) remain moister during grilling. And if you can find these "ribs" with the bone out, so much the better—you've essentially got a 1-inch-thick pork loin steak that grills beautifully.

TO PREPARE lemongrass, first peel it like a scallion. Virtually the entire inner core is tender enough to mince (in the winter, when the stalks have been in storage, you may have to peel off layer after layer to find the edible center). Figure a yield of about a tablespoon of minced lemongrass per stalk.

| Serve on a bed of shredded, lightly salted cabbage, tossed with chopped mint, lime juice, and black pepper to taste.

Slow-Cooked Ribs

This is a really easy dish that takes some time. But once you get it started (which will take just 5 minutes or so), you can all but ignore it during the cooking, just checking every now and then to turn the ribs and make sure the liquid doesn't dry out.

2 pounds pork spare ribs, cut into pieces, or beef short ribs

¼ cup plus 2 tablespoons soy sauce

1 star anise

1 dried chile

5 slices ginger (don't bother to peel)

2 garlic cloves, lightly crushed

2 teaspoons sugar

1 Combine the meat, ¼ cup soy sauce, star anise, chile, ginger, garlic, and sugar with ½ cup water in a skillet just broad enough to hold the meat.

2 Bring to a boil, then turn the heat to low, cover, and simmer for 2 hours or so, turning the meat occasionally and adding water, ½ cup at a time, if and when the pan dries out. The meat is done when it is tender and nearly falling from the bone. Remove the meat, spoon some or all of the juices over it, and serve.

WINE Beer, or a spicy red like Zinfandel

SERVE WITH Easy Rice (page 204) or Crisp Pan-Fried Noodle Cake (page 212)

SUGAR is key here. As it cooks, it makes the sauce not so much sweet but sticky.

IF YOU LIKE, you can remove the fat from the dish by separating the ribs and cooking liquid when the ribs are done. Refrigerate separately and skim the congealed fat from the liquid before combining and reheating.

Slow-Cooked Ribs with Vegetables: To make this into a whole-meal stew, increase the water to 2 cups and add some peeled and chunked carrots or turnips, whole pearl onions or shallots, or all of the above, after the meat has cooked for about an hour. Some shredded cabbage added during the last half hour or so of cooking is also good.

Pork Cutlet with Miso-Red Wine Sauce

TIME: 20 minutes
MAKES: 4 servings

In addition to its intense flavor, which is sweeter, saltier, and more complex than that of soy sauce, miso is a superb thickener, adding a rich, creamy consistency when whisked into a small amount of liquid. With that in mind, it's the work of a moment to turn the pan juices remaining after searing a piece of meat into a great sauce, using nothing more than miso and a little liquid. My choice here is pork for meat and red wine for liquid; the combination resulting from these three ingredients completely belies the amount of energy put into the dish.

Four 1-inch-thick bone-in pork chops, each about 6 ounces
Salt and freshly cracked black pepper
1 cup sturdy red wine, like Zinfandel or Cabernet Sauvignon
2 tablespoons red miso
¼ cup roughly chopped shiso, basil, or parsley, optional

1 Heat a heavy skillet over medium-high heat for 2 or 3 minutes, then add the chops. Sprinkle them with a little bit of salt and a lot of pepper, then brown them on one side for 4 to 5 minutes. Turn and brown the other side until firm and nearly cooked through, another 3 or 4 minutes. Transfer to a warm plate and turn the heat to medium.

2 Add the wine and cook, stirring occasionally with a wooden spoon to loosen any bits of meat that have stuck to the pan, until the wine reduces by about half. Turn the heat to low and add the miso; stir briskly to make a smooth mixture (a wire whisk will help here).

3 Taste the sauce and add more salt (unlikely) and pepper, if necessary. Spoon it over the pork, garnish with shiso if you like, and serve.

WINE The same as, or similar to, the wine you use to make the sauce

SERVE WITH Easy Rice (page 204) or Rice Salad with Peas and Soy (page 200); Green Salad with Soy Vinaigrette (page 197)

RED MISO (which is in fact brown) adds terrific color to the sauce and has the strongest flavor of all the misos; it also has the additional asset of being the easiest to find. Miso must be handled gently, because high heat practically destroys its flavor; so be sure to keep the heat low when you stir it in.

FOR THE pork, I prefer a bone-in chop, preferably from the rib end of the loin; it's a little bit fattier than other chops; these days, pork is so lean that the extra fat is a benefit rather than a detriment.

SHISO IS a Japanese herb (you've probably seen it with sushi) that is not easy to find; basil or even parsley are suitable substitutes here.

| Use boneless pork steaks from the loin or tenderloin or beef—rib-eye, strip, or skirt steaks are all fine. Reduce the cooking time slightly.

Forty-Minute Cassoulet

Cassoulet in 40 minutes or less is heresy, of course, but if you want the pleasure of serving something cassoulet-like without spending two days doing it, here you go. It's not "real" cassoulet, but glorified beans and meat. Like the original cassoulet it is a bean stew containing whatever meat, preferably fatty and flavorful, is available to throw in it. That's the spirit.

4 cups chopped tomatoes, with their juice (canned are fine)

1 tablespoon chopped garlic

4 cups white beans, nearly fully cooked, drained if canned (see above)

1 cup stock, dry red wine, bean-cooking liquid, or water

Salt

⅛ teaspoon cayenne, or to taste

1 pound Italian sausage, preferably in one piece

1 pound pork tenderloin, cut into 1-inch cubes

1 boned duck breast

1 Combine the tomatoes and garlic in a large saucepan and turn the heat to medium. Bring to a boil and add the beans. Bring to a boil again, stirring occasionally, then reduce the heat so the mixture bubbles regularly but not furiously. Cook for about 20 minutes, adding the liquid when the mixture becomes thick. Add the salt and cayenne when the beans are tender and flavorful.

2 Meanwhile, put the sausage in a skillet and turn the heat to medium-high; brown on both sides, turning only once or twice. Add the sausage to the tomato-bean mixture, along with the pork. Raise the heat a bit if necessary to keep a simmer going. Stir the beans occasionally so the pork chunks cook evenly; they'll finish cooking in the time it takes to prepare the duck.

3 Cut a ½-inch crosshatch pattern in the skin side of the duck breast, right down to the fat layer. Put the breast in the same skillet in which you cooked the sausage, skin side down, and turn the heat to medium-high. Cook

WINE Rough, inexpensive red from the south of France or elsewhere

SERVE WITH 60-Minute Bread (page 207) or good store-bought bread; Simple Green Salad (page 196)

until nicely browned, pouring any rendered duck fat and juices into the bean mixture. Turn the duck and brown the meat side, then crisp up the skin side again for a minute or so, once more pouring any juice into the beans. The total cooking time for the breast will be 6 to 8 minutes. When it is done, add the breast to the beans.

4 To serve, carve the sausage and duck breast into serving pieces, and put some on each of four to six plates. Top with beans and pork.

Keys To SUCCESS

UNLESS YOU have a lot of time, start with frozen beans, which are now being sold in most supermarkets. If you can't find frozen beans just use canned beans, but drain and rinse them first.

ALTHOUGH THE pork tenderloin need not be browned before further cooking, the sausage benefits from a quick browning, which is definitely worth the 5-minute effort.

IF YOU can get duck confit, just brown it lightly on both sides, adding both it and its fat to the stew in place of the duck breast.

With MINIMAL Effort

| Start with dried beans, cooked with a few sprigs of fresh thyme, ½ head of garlic, and a piece of salt pork or bacon.

| Cook the garlic in a little duck fat—don't let it brown—before adding the tomatoes and beans.

| Finish the dish by toasting some bread crumbs, seasoned with salt and pepper, in the fat remaining from browning the duck. Sprinkle these on top of the stew, then run it under the broiler to brown just before serving.

Grilled Lamb Ribs

Next to pork (spare) ribs, lamb ribs are the best down-and-dirty grill item I know. They're also the cheapest: Where I live, it's hard to pay more than a dollar a pound for them.

Like spare ribs, lamb ribs are the bones of the breast, separated into individual pieces. The supermarket meat department or butcher may give you the entire breast, or he may separate the ribs for you. If he does not, make sure to ask him to at least remove or cut through the breast-bone, which will make cutting in between the ribs fast and easy.

Grilled or Broiled Lamb Ribs

4 to 5 pounds lamb breast, cut into ribs	¼ cup honey, orange marmalade, or maple syrup
Salt and freshly ground black pepper	¼ cup Dijon mustard
	1 small onion, peeled

1 Start a charcoal or wood fire or preheat a gas grill to the maximum, or preheat a broiler; the fire should be only moderately hot and the rack should be at least 4 inches from the heat source. Bring a large pot of water to the boil; salt it. Put in the lamb and simmer for 10 minutes.

2 Drain the ribs. Grill or broil them for about 10 minutes, turning once or twice and sprinkling them with a little salt and pepper. Meanwhile, combine the honey, mustard, and onion in a blender and whiz until smooth.

3 When the ribs begin to brown, brush them with the sauce and continue to cook, watching carefully so they do not catch fire. When they are brown and crisp all over—a matter of no more than 10 or at the most 15 minutes—remove them from the grill and serve.

WINE Chianti, rough Zinfandel or Syrah
SERVE WITH Cornbread (page 209); Tomato Salad with Basil (page 198); baked beans; coleslaw

LAMB RIBS require special treatment while grilling, because they are loaded with fat (this is one of the reasons they taste so good, of course). You can grill them very slowly, or (my preference), parboil the ribs just for 10 minutes or so, long enough to render enough of the fat so that it doesn't catch fire the instant you put the ribs on the grill. You'll still need to be careful during grilling; don't leave the fire for more than a minute or two.

BROILING THEM makes this somewhat easier, but you still have to keep an eye out; left unattended, they will burn.

Lamb Ribs with Pesto: For the sauce, make a light pesto of basil, cilantro, or parsley, blending together about 2 tablespoons of olive oil to 1 cup of leaves, along with salt, a clove of garlic, and enough water to make the mixture creamy. Don't brush the ribs with this mixture, but pass it at the table.

Lamb Ribs with Salsa: Make Fast Tomato Salsa, page 199. Grill the ribs with just salt and pepper and pass the salsa at the table.

Lamb Ribs with Cucumber: Grill the ribs with just salt and pepper. Make a cucumber "salsa" by peeling, seeding, and chopping 2 cucumbers, then coarsely chopping them in a blender or food processor with mint and salt to taste. Pass at the table.

Lamb Ribs with Mango: Grill the ribs with just salt and pepper. Make a fast mango relish by combining the chopped flesh of 2 mangoes (or peaches) with ½ cup minced onion, the juice of 2 limes, and salt, pepper, and chopped cilantro to taste. Pass at the table.

| Rub the parboiled ribs with any spice rub, such as chili or curry powder, before grilling.

| Cook the ribs unadorned, then serve with a light drizzle of ½ cup fresh lemon juice and hot sauce and salt to taste.

Lamb with Peaches

A logical combination, and glorious once you taste it, with the sweet juice of the peaches deftly cutting through the richness of the lamb without being piercing. A hint of cinnamon (or an even smaller one of allspice—maybe ⅛ teaspoon) gives the dish a great aroma as it cooks and a slightly mysterious flavor at the table. And a pinch of cayenne or other red pepper makes a nice addition.

TIME: About 1½ hours, largely unattended
MAKES: 4 servings

Braised and Browned Lamb with Peaches

2 pounds boned shoulder of lamb, trimmed of fat and gristle and cut into 1- to 1½-inch pieces

Salt

1 cinnamon stick or ½ teaspoon ground cinnamon

¼ teaspoon cayenne or other red pepper or to taste

1 medium-to-large onion, cut in half

½ cup Port wine, red wine, or water

4 medium-to-large ripe peaches

Juice of 1 lemon

1 cup washed, dried, and roughly chopped fresh parsley

1 Place the lamb in a 12-inch skillet and turn the heat to medium-high. Season with salt and add the cinnamon, cayenne, onion, and wine. Bring to a boil, cover, and adjust the heat so that the mixture simmers steadily but not violently. Cook for 1 to 1½ hours, checking and stirring every 15 minutes or so, adding a little more liquid in the unlikely event that the mixture cooks dry. (This probably means that the heat is too high; turn it down a bit.)

2 When the meat is tender when poked with a small, sharp knife, remove the onion and cinnamon stick, then turn the heat to medium-high and cook off any remaining liquid, allowing the lamb to brown a little. Cut the peaches in half and remove their pits, then cut each of them into 12 or 16 wedges. Stir in the peaches and continue to cook, gently tossing or stirring the mixture, until the peaches are glazed and quite soft but still intact, about 5 minutes.

WINE Pinot Noir or California Merlot

SERVE WITH Easy Rice (page 204), rice pilaf, or Persian-style rice and potatoes; Simple Green Salad (page 196)

3 Stir in the lemon juice and most of the parsley; taste and adjust the seasoning. Garnish with the remaining bit of herb and serve.

| For a slightly more exotic dish, substitute fresh lime juice for the lemon and cilantro for the parsley.

Keys To SUCCESS

THIS IS a relatively fast and almost unattended braise, followed by finishing the dish in the same pan. Whereas most braises begin with browning, this one ends with it, reducing both spattering and time— since the lamb's liquid is mostly gone by the end of cooking, it doesn't go flying from the hot fat, and the meat browns faster. And the peaches, browning lightly in the same cooking liquid, contribute some of their juices to the pan while becoming meltingly tender.

Lamb with Peppers and Yogurt Sauce

TIME: 40 to 50 minutes
MAKES: 4 servings

You might think of this Turkish dish as a kind of lamb shish kebab with a couple of twists. First of all, it can be executed indoors (though in good weather, the initial browning could certainly be done on a grill). Second, it contains its own built-in sauce, a combination of yogurt and the juices exuded by lamb and roasted vegetables. The process is straightforward: You take large chunks of lamb and sear them. Then you roast peppers—a combination of both sweet and hot is ideal but not essential—and an onion. This is all combined with yogurt, then browned under the broiler before serving.

2 pounds boneless lamb (see Keys to Success) cut into 2-inch chunks

3 red or yellow bell peppers

2 or 3 chiles (see Keys to Success), optional

1 onion, peeled and halved

Salt and fresh ground black pepper

2 cups plain yogurt

1 Turn the heat to high under a cast-iron or other large heavy skillet for a couple of minutes. Add the lamb and quickly sear on all sides. Don't worry about cooking it through, but brown the exterior well, a couple of minutes per side.

2 Remove the lamb and put the peppers and chiles in the same skillet, still over high heat. Add the onion, cut sides down. Cook until the peppers blacken on all sides, 10 to 15 minutes, turning as necessary (the onion will blacken quickly; remove it and set aside). When the peppers are beginning to collapse, remove the skillet from the heat and cover with foil or a lid. Preheat the broiler, and adjust the rack so it is 2 to 4 inches from the heat source.

3 When the peppers cool slightly, peel and seed them, then cut or tear into strips; separate the onion into rings. Combine the peppers and onions with the lamb, salt, pepper, and yogurt in a roasting pan just large enough to hold the lamb in one layer. Broil until charred on top, just a few minutes, then serve.

WINE A rough red wine from southern France or Italy

SERVE WITH Pita bread or Easy Rice (page 204); Tomato Salad with Basil (page 198) or Simple Green Salad (page 196)

FOR THE lamb, you can use either leg or shoulder. Leg is leaner and best kept on the rare side; shoulder, which has more fat, can be cooked a little longer without drying out, which means it can be left under the broiler for a few extra minutes to give it an extra-crisp crust.

ANY ASSORTMENT of bell peppers is fine, preferably with the addition of one or two mildly hot peppers, such as Anaheims.

IT ONLY takes a couple of minutes to sear the lamb; so as long as you turn on an exhaust fan (and temporarily disconnect the smoke detector), you should be okay. The smoke produced by the searing peppers is in fact pleasantly fragrant.

| Sear a couple of skinned tomatoes along with (or after) the peppers; this only takes a minute or two and adds another level of flavor to the final sauce.

| Add a teaspoon or so of thyme leaves along with the yogurt.

| Serve the dish with lemon wedges or a sprinkling of chopped mint.

Boneless Lamb Shoulder Roast

Boneless Lamb Roast

Lamb shoulder is a bony cut of meat that can be turned easily into a boneless roast by someone who has the experience to do so. I'm not suggesting that you are that "someone"—neither am I—but that any butcher, including those who work in supermarkets, can and will perform this task quickly. The result is a round, tied piece of meat with lovely crevasses into which you can stick a simple seasoning mixture like garlic and parsley. This is a traditional combination for lamb, and rightly so, because the flavors marry so well.

1 cup washed and dried fresh parsley leaves

4 medium or 2 large garlic cloves

Salt and freshly ground black pepper

2 tablespoons extra virgin olive oil, more or less

One 3- to 4-pound boned lamb shoulder

1 Preheat the oven to 300°F. (Line a pan with foil to facilitate cleanup if you like). Mince together the parsley and garlic until quite fine (a small food processor will work for this). Add a big pinch of salt and some pepper and enough olive oil to make a slurry. Smear this on and into the lamb, making sure to get it in every nook and cranny you can reach. Put the lamb in the roasting pan.

2 Roast for about 1½ hours, basting with the pan juices every 30 minutes or so. When the internal temperature reaches 140°F, turn the heat to 400°F and roast for about 10 minutes more, or until the internal temperature is 150°F and the exterior has browned nicely.

3 Let the roast sit for about 10 minutes before carving, then carve and serve, with some of the juices that come out during carving.

WINE Fine Burgundy or Bordeaux, or a good Rioja

SERVE WITH Mashed Potatoes (page 205) or Crisp Potatoes (page 206); Tomato Salad with Basil (page 198); Sautéed Shiitake Mushrooms (page 202) or Steamed Broccoli (or Other Vegetable) (page 203)

THERE IS no denying that the shoulder is fatty, so ask the butcher to remove as much surface fat as possible while he is trimming the meat. (It pays to phone ahead, or to plan to spend a while shopping while the butcher does his thing.) Most shoulders weigh in at 3 to 4 pounds after boning, making this roast enough to serve at least six people.

AS LONG as the temperature is kept relatively low—it's best to roast the shoulder at 300°F—roasting renders the fat just as well as braising. A short boost of the oven heat during the last 15 minutes or so of roasting guarantees a beautifully browned, crisp exterior. The ideal degree of doneness is just short of well done, a stage at which the meat achieves the best combination of tenderness, flavor, and leanness.

Boneless Lamb Roast with Coriander Seeds:
Along with the parsley and garlic, use 2 tablespoons of crushed coriander seeds. Put them in a plastic bag and pound gently with a rolling pin, rubber mallet, or like object to crush them.

Boneless Lamb Roast with Provençal Flavors:
In place of the parsley, use 1 tablespoon minced fresh rosemary leaves or 1 teaspoon dried rosemary or lavender, 3 or 4 minced anchovy fillets (optional), and 2 tablespoons olive (or anchovy) oil, along with the garlic.

Grilled Boneless Leg of Lamb

There may be no meat better for grilling than boneless leg of lamb. It cooks reasonably quickly, usually in less than half an hour, but still develops an irresistibly crunchy crust. Even better, that crust can be flavored in minutes before it is cooked with any of a dozen combinations of seasonings. Marinating is unnecessary, as the meat itself has exquisite flavor and really needs no more than salt.

One 3- to 4-pound butterflied leg of lamb
1 tablespoon olive oil
1 teaspoon minced garlic
1 tablespoon minced fresh rosemary, or 2 teaspoons dried
1 tablespoon chopped or crushed fennel seeds
Salt and freshly ground black pepper

1 Start a charcoal or wood fire, preheat a gas grill to the maximum, or preheat the broiler. The fire should be quite hot, and the rack set 4 inches from heat source.

2 Trim the lamb of excess fat. Mix together the oil, garlic, rosemary, fennel seeds, salt, and pepper; thoroughly rub this mixture into the lamb, making sure to get some into all the crevices. (If time allows, it does no harm to let the prepared lamb sit in the refrigerator for up to 24 hours; just return the meat to room temperature before grilling.)

3 Sear the meat over the hottest part of the grill until nicely browned on both sides, 10 to 15 minutes. Continue to cook with the grill (you can cover the grill to speed things up a bit) for 5 to 15 minutes longer, until the internal temperature at the thickest part is about 125°F. Let the meat rest for 5 minutes before slicing and serving.

WINE Bordeaux or another big red
SERVE WITH Raw Beet Salad (page 194), Simple Green Salad (page 196), Tomato Salad with Basil (page 198), Green Salad with Soy Vinaigrette (page 197); Steamed Broccoli (or Other Vegetable) (page 203), Roasted Peppers (page 195), and/or Glazed Carrots (page 201)

THERE IS no need to do the boning yourself, as there once was; nearly every supermarket carries boned leg of lamb. Most pieces are big enough to serve six, and often ten.

THE LEG'S irregular shape virtually guarantees that every eater will be happy—lamb is the only meat good at every stage of doneness. When the thickest parts have cooked to rare, the ends will be well done, the parts in between medium.

BONELESS LEGS sold in supermarkets are sometimes wrapped in an elastic net to form them into a round roast. For grilling, remove this so the meat lies flat. If the larger end of the meat is 3 or more inches thick, you might cut a flap to make that lobe thinner and flatter so that it cooks more evenly. Using a sharp, thin-bladed knife and working from the side of the lobe that faces the rest of the meat, make a horizontal cut about halfway down from top to bottom, most of the way through, and fold the meat out; in essence, you are butterflying the butterfly.

Grilled Boneless Leg of Lamb with Coriander and Ginger: Instead of the oil-rosemary mixture, use a combination of 1 tablespoon coriander seeds, 1 teaspoon black peppercorns, 1 tablespoon garlic, and 1 tablespoon fresh ginger, all minced or coarsely ground together; moisten with a little soy sauce.

Curried Boneless Leg of Lamb: Instead of the oil-rosemary mixture, rub the lamb all over with 2 tablespoons curry powder mixed with ½ cup yogurt.

Broiled or Roasted Boneless Leg of Lamb: Adjust the broiler rack so that it sits 4 to 6 inches from the heat source. Keep an eye on it to prevent burning; the broiling time will be about 30 minutes. Or roast it in the middle of the oven, at 450°F, turning occasionally; the cooking time will be about 40 minutes.

| Substitute 2 teaspoons fresh thyme (or 1 teaspoon dried) for the fennel seeds.

| Use 1 tablespoon soy sauce or 1 tablespoon minced anchovies instead of the salt.

Salads and Side Dishes

Raw
Beet Salad

Eaten raw, beets are delicious; even self-proclaimed beet-haters will like them in this salad. To eat a beet raw, you have to peel it and shred it. The first step is easiest with a regular vegetable peeler. I do the second with the metal blade of a food processor, pulsing the machine on and off until the beets are finely cut. You can use the shredding blade, but it isn't any easier or better. Or you can use a manual grater, but only if you're interested in an upper-body workout.

1 pound beets

1 large shallot

Salt and freshly ground black pepper

2 teaspoons Dijon mustard, or to taste

1 tablespoon extra virgin olive oil

2 tablespoons sherry vinegar or other good strong vinegar

About 1 tablespoon minced parsley, dill, or chervil; or about 1 teaspoon minced rosemary or tarragon

1 Peel the beets and the shallot. Combine them in the bowl of a food processor fitted with a metal blade, and pulse carefully until the beets are shredded; do not purée. (Or grate the beets by hand and mince the shallots; combine.) Scrape into a bowl.

2 Toss with the salt, pepper, mustard, oil, and vinegar. Taste and adjust the seasoning. Toss in the herbs and serve.

Roasted
Peppers

Roasting gives amazing depth to vegetables, and especially peppers. The simplest way to serve these is to drizzle them with extra virgin olive oil, along with some salt and pepper, but you can also add a few drops of vinegar. The next step is to garnish with anchovies, capers, and/or herbs.

4 large red bell peppers (about 2 pounds)

Salt and freshly ground black pepper

2 tablespoons extra virgin olive oil

1 Preheat the oven to 500°F. Line a roasting pan with enough foil to later fold over the top. Place the peppers in the pan. Roast, turning the peppers about every 10 minutes, until the peppers collapse, about 40 minutes.

2 Fold the foil over the peppers and allow them to cool. Working over a bowl, remove the core, skin, and seeds from each of the peppers. It's okay if the peppers naturally fall into strips during this process. Sprinkle with salt, pepper, and oil and serve at room temperature. (You can refrigerate these, tightly wrapped or covered, for a few days; bring to room temperature before serving.)

Simple Green Salad

Many people are hooked on premade salad dressing because they believe that homemade dressing is a production, but it need not be. Try this.

4 to 6 cups trimmed, washed, dried and torn assorted greens

¼ to ⅓ cup extra virgin olive oil

1 to 2 tablespoons balsamic vinegar or sherry vinegar, or fresh lemon juice to taste

Salt

Freshly ground black pepper, optional

1 Place the greens in a bowl and drizzle them with oil, vinegar, and a pinch of salt. Toss and taste. Correct the seasoning, add pepper if desired, and serve immediately.

Green Salad with Soy Vinaigrette

TIME: 10 minutes
MAKES: 4 servings

This is a great salad with arugula, watercress, or mixed greens—you can even include some raw chopped kale, red cabbage, or shredded broccoli. Their strong flavors are perfect with the mild sweetness of the dressing.

About 6 cups greens, trimmed, washed, and dried

3 tablespoons rice or wine vinegar

3 tablespoons soy sauce

½ teaspoon sugar

¼ teaspoon cayenne

1 teaspoon toasted sesame oil

Salt, optional

1 Place the greens in a bowl. Mix together the vinegar, soy sauce, sugar, cayenne, and oil and dress the greens with this mixture.

2 Toss, then taste and add salt and more of any other seasoning if necessary. Serve.

Tomato Salad with Basil

So few ingredients, and so much flavor—as long as the ingredients are of high quality! Omit the basil if you can't find any, but where there are good tomatoes there is probably good basil. Add slices of mozzarella to make this more substantial.

4 perfectly ripe medium tomatoes

Salt and freshly ground black pepper

A handful of washed, dried, and roughly chopped basil

Extra virgin olive oil

1 Core the tomatoes (cut a cone-shaped wedge out of the stem end), and cut them into slices about ¼ inch thick.

2 Lay the tomatoes on a platter or four individual plates. Sprinkle with salt, pepper, and basil. Drizzle with oil and serve.

Fast Tomato Salsa

You can make this hot or not, as you like; it's a good use for less-than-perfect tomatoes and a fine side dish for anything grilled.

4 medium tomatoes
½ cup chopped scallions
1 garlic clove, minced
2 tablespoons fresh lime juice
Salt and freshly ground black pepper

Minced chiles or crushed red pepper flakes, optional
½ cup washed, dried, and chopped cilantro leaves

1 Core the tomatoes (cut a cone-shaped wedge out of the stem end), and chop them. Toss them with the scallions, garlic, lime juice, salt, pepper, and chiles if you like. Set aside until you're ready to eat, or for about an hour.
2 Toss in the cilantro and serve.

Rice Salad with Peas and Soy

TIME: 30 to 40 minutes
MAKES: 4 to 6 servings

You can use any short- or medium-grained rice you like for this dish, which is most easily made with left-over rice. Substitute shelled *edamame* (fresh or frozen soybeans) for the peas if you like.

Salt
½ cup fresh or frozen peas
1 cup Arborio rice
¼ cup minced shallot
¼ cup fresh lime juice, plus more as needed

2 tablespoons peanut, grape-seed, corn, or other light oil
2 tablespoons good soy sauce
¼ cup minced fresh cilantro leaves
Freshly ground black pepper

1 Bring a small pot of water to a boil. Bring a large pot of water to a boil. When the small pot comes to a boil, salt it. Add the peas and cook for about 2 minutes, or until the peas lose their raw flavor. Drain and rinse in cold water to stop the cooking. Drain and set aside.

2 When the large pot of water comes to a boil, salt it. Add the rice and cook, stirring, until it is completely tender, about 15 minutes. Drain the rice and rinse it quickly under cold water to stop the cooking, but don't chill it entirely.

3 Stir the shallot into the rice and mix well. Add the lime juice, oil, and soy, and mix well again. Add the cilantro, peas, and pepper, and mix. Taste and add more lime juice, soy, or pepper as needed. Serve immediately or refrigerate, well covered, for up to a day; bring back to room temperature before serving.

Glazed Carrots

TIME: 30 to 40 minutes

MAKES: 4 servings

This easy, fast cooking process turns carrots into a luxury vegetable. For even better flavor, add the grated zest of an orange or lemon when about 5 minutes of cooking time remain.

1 pound carrots, cut into ½- to 1-inch chunks

Salt

2 tablespoons (¼ stick) butter

Chopped parsley, chervil, or mint, optional

1 Combine the carrots in a saucepan with a pinch of salt. Add water to half cover the carrots. Add the butter, cover the pan, and turn the heat to medium-high.

2 Simmer until the carrots are nearly tender, about 20 minutes. Uncover; much of the water will have evaporated. Continue to cook until the carrots are shiny; if they threaten to burn, add 1 to 2 tablespoons water. When the carrots are done, taste and adjust the seasoning if necessary. Garnish with parsley, if you like, and serve.

Sautéed Shiitake Mushrooms

I know portobello mushrooms are all the rage, but shiitakes are the closest thing you can find to wild mushrooms without spending a fortune or foraging in the woods. To me, they are invaluable, and prepared in this simple, traditional way, they are spectacular.

¼ cup extra virgin olive oil

1 pound shiitakes, trimmed of their stems (which can be reserved for stock, but are too tough to eat) and sliced

Salt and freshly ground black pepper

1 teaspoon minced garlic or 2 tablespoons chopped shallots

Chopped fresh parsley, optional

1 Pour the oil into a large skillet over medium heat. When it is hot, add the mushrooms, then some salt and pepper. Cook, stirring occasionally, until the mushrooms are tender, 10 to 15 minutes.

2 Add the garlic and turn the heat to high. Cook, stirring occasionally, until the mushrooms begin to brown and become crisp at the edge, about 10 minutes. Taste and adjust the seasoning if necessary, garnish with the parsley if you like, and serve hot or at room temperature.

Steamed Broccoli
(or Other Vegetable)

TIME: About 20 minutes
MAKES: 4 servings

This is a technique that will work for most vegetables. You can either steam or boil the vegetable and serve it directly from the pot, or rinse it under cold water, then reheat and serve it later.

1 pound broccoli or other vegetable
Salt

Fresh lemon juice, soy sauce, melted butter, or extra virgin olive oil

1 Trim the broccoli as necessary (the thick stems should be peeled with a vegetable peeler or paring knife to make them less tough). Cut into equal size pieces. Steam over boiling water (or boil in salted water to cover) until tender and bright green, usually less than 10 minutes.
2 Drain if necessary, sprinkle with salt, and drizzle with any liquid seasoning you choose (including melted butter if you like). Or run under cold water and refrigerate. To reheat, put a little olive oil or butter in a pan over medium heat and turn the vegetable in it until hot; season to taste and serve.

Easy
Rice

This is a fast and ridiculously easy way to make rice, and it works. It also produces rice that keeps well in the pot for a long time.

1½ cups long-, medium-, or short-grain rice, rinsed and drained

2½ cups water
1 teaspoon salt, or to taste

1 Combine all the ingredients in a medium saucepan and bring to a boil over medium-high heat. When the water starts boiling, stir and lower the heat to medium, so that it still bubbles but not furiously.

2 After 8 to 12 minutes, small craters will appear on the surface of the rice, indicating that the water is almost all absorbed. Cover the pot, turn the heat to low, and cook until tender, about 5 more minutes. Serve immediately or let the rice sit for up to an hour before serving.

Mashed Potatoes

TIME: About 40 minutes

MAKES: 4 servings

Mashed potatoes are easy to make. If you like them lumpy, mash them with a fork or potato masher; if you like them creamy, use a food mill or ricer. If you like them lean, omit the butter and substitute some of the potato cooking water for the milk.

2 pounds baking potatoes, such as Idaho or russet, peeled and cut into quarters

3 tablespoons butter or extra virgin olive oil

¾ cup milk, gently warmed

Salt and freshly ground black pepper

1 Boil the potatoes in a pot with salted water to cover until soft; this will take about 30 minutes.

2 When the potatoes are done, drain them, then mash them well or put them through a food mill. Return them to the pot over very low heat and stir in the butter and—gradually—the milk, beating with a wooden spoon until smooth and creamy. Season with salt and pepper as necessary. Serve immediately, keep warm, or reheat in a microwave.

Crisp
Potatoes

The late, great Pierre Franey—author of *The 60-Minute Gourmet*—showed me how to make these twenty years ago (of course he used butter), and I have been making them weekly ever since.

1½ to 2 pounds waxy red or white potatoes, peeled and cut into ½- to 1-inch cubes

¼ cup extra virgin olive oil, more or less

1 teaspoon minced garlic

Salt and freshly ground black pepper

1 Add the potatoes to a pot of salted water, bring to a boil, and simmer until nearly tender, 10 to 15 minutes. Drain well.

2 Heat the oil over medium-high heat in a 12-inch non-stick skillet for 3 or 4 minutes. You can use more oil for crisper potatoes, or less oil to cut the fat. (You can also use butter, if you prefer, or a combination.) Add the potatoes along with a healthy sprinkling of salt and pepper, and cook, tossing and stirring from time to time (not constantly), until they are nicely browned all over, 10 to 20 minutes.

3 Add the garlic and continue to cook for 5 more minutes, stirring frequently. Taste and adjust the seasoning if necessary, and serve.

60-Minute Bread

TIME: 1 to 2 hours, largely unattended

MAKES: 1 loaf

I won't claim that this is the best bread you've ever eaten, but it's the fastest yeast-risen bread imaginable, and it's better than anything you can buy in my supermarket. Nor does it take much of your attention.

3 cups all-purpose flour, plus more as needed

2 teaspoons instant yeast, such as SAF

2 teaspoons salt

1 Combine the flour, yeast, and salt in a bowl or food processor. Add 1¼ cups warm water all at once, stirring with a wooden spoon or mixing with the machine on. Continue to mix, for a minute or two longer by hand, about 30 seconds total with the food processor. Add additional water by the tablespoon if necessary, until a ball forms.

2 Shape the dough into a flat round or long loaf, adding only enough flour to allow you to handle the dough. Place the dough on a baking sheet or a well-floured pizza peel. Let it rise in the warmest place in your kitchen, covered, while you preheat the oven to 425°F. (If you have time, let it rise for an hour or so.)

3 Bake the bread on a sheet, or slide it onto a baking stone. Bake until done, 30 to 45 minutes; the crust will be golden-brown, crisp, and firm.

Olive Oil Croutons

A crouton is not only a little cube of bread you use in salads or for stuffing, it is also a perfectly toasted slice that makes a wonderful side dish. The perfect use for stale bread.

¼ cup extra virgin olive oil, butter, or a combination

1 garlic clove, smashed and peeled

4 thick slices good bread

Salt

1 Pour the oil into a large skillet and turn the heat to medium-low. Add the garlic and cook, turning occasionally, until it is lightly browned, less than 5 minutes.

2 Add the bread slices and cook, turning occasionally and adjusting the heat so they brown nicely, 2 or 3 minutes per side. Remove and sprinkle lightly with salt; serve hot or at room temperature.

Cornbread

Cornbread is a quick bread—that is, risen with baking powder, no yeast—and the most useful one of all.

Everyone loves it, too.

1¼ cups buttermilk, milk, or yogurt

2 tablespoons (¼ stick) butter or olive oil

1½ cups cornmeal

½ cup flour

1½ teaspoons baking powder

1 teaspoon salt

2 tablespoons sugar

1 egg

1 Preheat the oven to 375°F. Put the butter in a medium ovenproof skillet (nonstick or well-seasoned) or in an 8-inch square baking pan over medium heat; heat until good and hot, about 2 minutes, then turn off the heat.

2 Meanwhile, combine the cornmeal, flour, baking powder, and salt in a bowl. Mix the egg into the buttermilk. Stir the buttermilk mixture into the dry ingredients, combining well; if it seems too dry, add another 1 to 2 tablespoons milk. Pour the batter into the preheated fat, shake the pan once or twice, and place it in the oven.

3 Bake for about 30 minutes, until the top is lightly browned and the sides have pulled away from the pan; a toothpick inserted into the center will come out clean. Serve hot or warm.

Cold Noodles with Sesame Sauce

TIME: About 40 minutes
MAKES: 4 to 6 servings

One of the best make-in-advance side dishes, and a plus at almost any buffet. Not bad as a main course, either, especially if you shred some cooked chicken into it.

12 ounces fresh Chinese egg noodles or dried pasta

2 tablespoons toasted sesame oil

½ cup sesame paste (tahini) or natural peanut butter

1 tablespoon sugar

¼ cup soy sauce

1 tablespoon rice or wine vinegar

Tabasco or other hot sauce

Salt and freshly ground black pepper

At least ½ cup minced scallions

1 Cook the noodles in boiling salted water until they are tender, but not mushy. Drain, then rinse in cold water for a minute or two. Toss with 1 tablespoon of the oil and refrigerate for up to 2 hours, or proceed with the recipe.

2 Beat together the tahini, sugar, soy sauce, vinegar, and remaining 1 tablespoon oil. Add a little hot sauce and salt and pepper; taste and adjust the seasoning as necessary. Thin the sauce with hot water, so that it is about the consistency of heavy cream.

3 Toss together the noodles and the sauce, and add more of any seasoning if necessary. Garnish with the scallions and serve.

Coconut Rice and Beans

TIME: About 30 minutes (with precooked beans)

MAKES: 4 to 6 servings

A staple in the Caribbean, this is sweet and filling. If you use canned beans, discard the canning liquid and rinse them before using.

1 to 2 cups cooked or canned red beans, with their cooking liquid (if any)

1½ cups rice, preferably long-grain

One 12- to 14-ounce can (1½ to 2 cups) unsweetened

coconut milk or 2 cups homemade coconut milk (page 45)

Salt and freshly ground black pepper

1 Place the beans in a medium saucepan; turn the heat to medium-high, and, if there is any liquid, cook most of it out, stirring occasionally.

2 Add the rice and the coconut milk to the beans. Cover and turn the heat to low. Cook for about 20 minutes, or until the rice is tender and the liquid is absorbed. If necessary, add a bit of boiling water to finish the cooking; it is more likely that you will need to uncover and raise the heat to medium-high to cook out excess liquid. Season with salt and pepper and serve.

Crisp Pan-Fried Noodle Cake

TIME: 30 to 40 minutes
MAKES: 4 to 6 servings

An unusual and terrific alternative to rice with stir-fries or any moist dish, and delicious by itself.

1 pound fresh Chinese egg noodles, or 12 ounces dried pasta

½ cup minced scallions

2 tablespoons soy sauce

3 to 4 tablespoons peanut or vegetable oil

1 Bring a large pot of water to a boil; cook the noodles until they are tender, but not mushy. Drain, then toss with the scallions, soy sauce, and 1 tablespoon of the oil.

2 Pour 2 tablespoons of the oil into a heavy medium to large skillet, preferably nonstick; turn the heat to medium-high. When the oil is hot, add the noodle mix, spreading it out evenly and pressing it down.

3 Cook for 2 minutes, then turn the heat to medium-low. Continue to cook until the cake is holding together and is nicely browned on the bottom, about 10 minutes. Turn carefully; the easiest way to do this is to slide the cake out onto a plate, cover it with another plate, invert the plates, and slide the cake back into the skillet, browned side up (add the remaining 1 tablespoon oil to the skillet if necessary).

4 Cook on the other side until brown. Cut into eighths or quarters and serve.

Index